MW01168493

LIFE MATTERS

SO LET'S

EAT LIKE IT

THE FAMILY COOKBOOK

---

62 MOUTHWATERING NATURALITE RECIPES

JABEZ EL ISRAEL

CO-AUTHORED BY: THE ISRAEL FAMILY

GREETINGS FROM THE ISRAEL FAMILY!

If you're reading these words, we want you to know you are greatly appreciated. It is truly a pleasure for us to share some of our favorite family recipes with you and yours. All we ask is that when you prepare these meals for yourself and your loved ones, that you prepare them with love in your heart.

Preparing meals can be viewed as a mechanical action. We don't view it as such. We have realized that when we prepare meals while we're in a good mood, the food always tastes better. There is definitely something about it. Think about all the things that you love about yourself and about the people that you are preparing the meal for. Not only will you be able to taste the difference, but it will also settle into your mind the importance of making sure the ingredients are good for you, as well as the people you are preparing the meal for.

We've designed this cookbook to help people lose weight. Every recipe is compatible with the principles laid out in my book "Life Matters So Let's Eat Like It!" If you haven't read the book yet, it is a book of simple, yet very effective principles that anyone can follow if they have a desire to lose weight and/or be healthier.

If you had to sum up "Life Matters So Let's Eat Like It!" in a few words, it would go something like this: We are natural beings, so our bodies are compatible with natural things. So, **eat natural!** The only way to know if something is natural is to know the ingredients. So **read the ingredients!**

We understand that this is a big world with a lot of different ways of looking at eating. So naturally there are a lot of different choices being made. Some people choose to eat whatever they have a taste for. Others might avoid gluten or consider themselves a vegan or a vegetarian. Then, there are others that choose to eat mostly meat. Maybe you consider yourself a pescatarian or maybe you eat only raw fruits and vegetables. The list goes on and on. We want to meet you where you're at and we want to meet you in the healthiest way possible. So, we have recipes in this book for everyone!

It's Important to note that the recipes in this cookbook that contain meat, can also be prepared without it. We've designed this recipe book intentionally to help the principles of "Life Matters So Let's Eat Like It!" settle into whoever's mind that is utilizing it. In my honest opinion, unless we're eating only raw fruits and vegetables, we can be eating better. It's also our opinion that it's not that easy to jump to just eating raw fruits and vegetables. So this book is designed to highlight easy steps in the right direction. The most important part in achieving a desired outcome is knowing the location of the outcome. When we know the location, we can move in the right direction. The Israel family cookbook is a cookbook designed like a roadmap to a specific location. The location being our natural body size and optimal health!

We pray these meals bring joy into your household. We pray the act of preparing them will guide you into a deeper understanding of consumption and the benefits of consuming consciously.

Prayers Up Blessings Up!

The Israel Family

"I've noticed the closer I look at my blessings, the BIGGER they get!"

—Jabez el Israel

OUR PRAYERS FOR YOU...

<u>MEKHI:</u> I wish you have a healthy and successful life.

<u>SUPREME:</u> I pray that this book really changes your life. I pray that if one of your family members are not eating healthy, that you give this cookbook to them to inspire them to make a change. Finally, I pray for you to have a happy and successful life.

<u>BUDDA:</u> I pray for your soul that you achieve happiness and complete bliss in your coming times, letting your happiness pass onto others around you.

<u>JACINDA:</u> I pray that anything that you put your mind to, you are able to accomplish in life.

<u>SHANIYA:</u> I pray that this cookbook helps you accomplish your goal to be healthier.

<u>NICOLE:</u> I pray that you all are blessed with an infinite desire to be better in order to live a longer, more joyous life. Make the decision to get 1% better every day.

<u>JABEZ:</u> I pray that continuous self-improvement ignites in your soul. I also pray your life is full of success, happiness, health, and the desire to be a moral person that uplifts and brings value to everyone around you! Prayers up blessings up!

From left to right: Supreme, Jacinda,
Shaniya, Mekhi, Budda, Nicole, Jabez

"The time is always right to do what is right."

—Martin Luther King Jr.

TABLE OF CONTENTS

DESSERTS 175

ROOTED IN NATURE:

The Naturalite Foundations of Our Family Cookbook 4-Part Video Series

Scan QR Codes Below to Watch the Videos:

**Cooking
with Intention**

**Tradition
in a Bag**

**Shopping
with Sense**

**Honoring
Our Origins**

WHAT IS A NATURALITE?

A Naturalite is someone who chooses to be aware of what's in their food by reading the ingredients and choosing natural food options, prioritizing what's free from heavily processed ingredients and harmful chemicals. The focus of a Naturalite is clear: to reconnect with nature and honor the wisdom of God's design in the way we eat. While vegans eliminate animal products, Naturalites eliminate processed foods and chemicals. We prioritize consuming foods in their natural form. Some Naturalites eat meat, while others don't, but all embrace the dietary guidelines laid out in the book of Leviticus, recognizing the wisdom in choosing clean animal flesh when it aligns with these biblical principles.

The Naturalite mission doesn't stop at natural weight loss. It extends into agriculture and how we interact with the earth itself. My next book, *The More We Grow, the More We'll See Everything We Need is Free*, makes growing natural food simple by focusing on four foundational principles: soil, sunlight, climate, and water. Like weight loss, growing food has been overcomplicated. This book was designed to make it simple. It's about learning how to grow food naturally and abundantly, without chemicals, for free! It's about planting seeds—literally and figuratively—for a better future. From the fruits and vegetables we cultivate to the trees we plant through my Jabez Mango Seeds initiative, this lifestyle is a movement toward wellness, sustainability, and community.

Imagine a world where our food choices heal both our bodies and the earth, where communities are built on the principles of giving back to nature and supporting one another. That's the heart of being a Naturalite. It's not just a diet—it's a way of life that prioritizes wholeness, connection, and respect for creation.

If you've embraced the teachings of this book, then you've already taken the first steps toward living as a Naturalite. Together, we can continue this journey—because when we align with nature, we align with something much bigger than ourselves. This is more than a lifestyle; it's a legacy we can leave behind, one choice at a time.

TAKE THE NEXT STEP

This book is more than a collection of recipes—it's a celebration of family, love, and the joy of nourishing those we care about. Each recipe in these pages has been a favorite in our home, and we hope they bring just as much joy and connection to your family as they have to ours. We created this cookbook with you in mind, knowing that the meals we share can become cherished traditions and a foundation for healthier, happier lives.

We're excited to let you know that beyond these recipes, we've created opportunities and resources to help you continue your journey toward natural living, delicious eating, and achieving even more. Whether it's exploring other tools and products we've developed, joining a community of like-minded people or discovering new ways to thrive, we're here to support you every step of the way.

To explore everything we've put together for you, simply open your phone's camera, point it at the QR code, and tap the link that appears on your screen. There, you'll find valuable resources, products, and opportunities designed to enhance your journey and help you create a life you'll love.

We're excited to grow with you—because when you thrive, the world becomes a better place. As you explore these recipes and take the next step with us, know that you're part of a movement that's bringing natural living, joy, and wellness back to the heart of our lives. Let's grow together!

"You must eat to live, not live to eat."

Dr. Sebi

BREAKFAST

Vanilla & Blueberry Waffles (Non-Dairy)

VANILLA & BLUEBERRY WAFFLES (NON-DAIRY)

YIELDS: 5-8 WAFFLES
PREP TIME: 5 MINS
COOK TIME: 15 MINS

INGREDIENTS

1-3/4 cup non bleached unenriched all-purpose flour

1 tbsp baking powder

3 tbsp raw cane sugar

¼ tsp all-natural coarse salt

1-½ cup all-natural non-dairy milk (preferably with vanilla flavor) (Ex. Almond milk or coconut milk)

2 large brown eggs

6 tbsp extra virgin olive oil

1 tsp pure vanilla extract (if didn't use vanilla flavored milk)

½ cup blueberries, cut in half

DIRECTIONS

1. Preheat waffle maker. Lightly grease with a little olive oil or coconut oil.

2. In a medium bowl, whisk together flour, baking powder, sugar and salt.

3. Add milk, eggs, olive oil and vanilla extract. Whisk until batter is smooth. Stir in blueberries.

4. Add batter to waffle maker. Usually about ¾ cup. (Check waffle maker instructions for amount of batter per waffle)

5. Cook per instructions for your waffle maker.

6. Immediately serve and savor!

Sunshine Breakfast Bowl

SUNSHINE BREAKFAST BOWL

SERVINGS: 2-3
PREP TIME: 10 MINS
COOK TIME: 5 MINS

INGREDIENTS

1 cup Polenta grits

3 cups spring water

2 tsp all-natural coarse salt

¼ tsp virgin unrefined coconut oil

2 cups lettuce, spinach or spring mix, thinly chopped

¼ cup cilantro

1/3 cup sweet onion, thinly sliced

5-7 grape tomatoes, cut into fourths

1 avocado, pitted and cubed

1 tbsp extra virgin olive oil

½ tsp red pepper flakes (optional, to your liking)

1 tsp French herb blend

½ lemon, squeezed

½ tsp parsley

DIRECTIONS

1. In a medium saucepan, bring water to a boil.

2. Add polenta grits and salt. Stir well and lower heat to low. Cover with lid. Cook for 5 minutes. Stir well every 2 minutes to prevent clumping.

3. Once done cooking, remove from heat. Add a tbsp of spring water to grits until you reach your desired consistency.

4. Add coconut oil and stir.

5. Prepare salad mixture in medium bowl. Add lettuce, spinach or spring mix, cilantro, onion, grape tomatoes, avocado, olive oil, red pepper flakes and French herb blend.

6. Plate grits then top with salad mixture. Squeeze lemon on top and add parsley.

7. Serve and savor!

Wholesome Wheat Wonders (Non-Dairy)

WHOLESOME WHEAT WONDERS (NON-DAIRY)

YIELDS: 10 PANCAKES
PREP TIME: 5 MINS
COOK TIME: 20 MINS

INGREDIENTS

1-½ cup spring water

½ cup virgin unrefined coconut oil, melted

2 large brown eggs

2 tsp pure vanilla extract

2-¼ cups + 2 tbsp non-enriched unbleached all-purpose flour

¼ cup raw cane sugar

3 tbsp baking powder

1 tsp all-natural cracked sea salt

Grapeseed oil, to grease skillet

DIRECTIONS

1. In a medium bowl, add water, coconut oil, eggs and vanilla. Mix well.

2. In a separate medium sized bowl, add flour, sugar, baking powder and salt. Mix well.

3. Add dry mix to the wet mix and stir until well combined. (DO NOT OVER-MIX)

4. Grease non-stick skillet with a little grapeseed oil or coconut oil and turn stove on medium heat.

5. Pour batter into middle of pan for even cooking.

6. Cook until you see bubbling on the pancake. Gently lift pancake. If the bottom is golden brown, carefully flip to other side. Cook that side until golden brown.

7. Serve and savor!

Avocado Slice of Paradise

AVOCADO SLICE OF PARADISE

SERVINGS: 2 SLICES
PREP TIME: 15 MINS
COOK TIME: N/A

INGREDIENTS

Bread of choice (non-enriched, unbleached and all-natural)

1 ripe avocado, peeled and pitted

1 tsp all-natural coarse salt

½ tsp cracked black pepper

½ tsp onion powder

½ tsp garlic powder

2 cups baby spinach, chopped

¼ small, sweet onion, thinly sliced

¼ small bell pepper, thinly sliced (any color)

2 tbsp all-natural sun-dried tomatoes, minced

5 grape tomatoes, cut into fourths

1 tbsp all-natural Jalapeños or our homemade jalapeño recipe, minced (optional)

1 tsp all-natural balsamic vinegar

1 tsp red pepper flakes (optional)

½ tsp French herb blend

¼ cup chopped walnuts (optional)

1-½ tsp extra virgin olive oil

DIRECTIONS

1. In a small bowl, add avocado, ½ tsp salt, ½ tsp pepper, ½ tsp garlic powder and ½ tsp onion powder. Use fork to smash and break up avocado. Mix until seasonings are well combined.

2. In another small bowl, mix together spinach, onions, bell peppers, sun dried tomatoes, grape tomatoes, jalapeños, balsamic vinegar, ½ tsp salt, 1 tsp red pepper flakes, ½ tsp French herb blend and olive oil.

3. Toast bread to your liking.

4. Top toast with avocado spread.

5. Top avocado spread with salad mixture.

6. Top salad mixture with walnuts (optional).

7. Serve and savor!

NOTE: Best topped with our Garlic Cilantro Sauce. You can also use our Homemade Jalapeño recipe for the jalapeños.

"Your body is a reflection of what you eat. If you want a better body, make better food choices."

—Dr. Llaila Afrika

The Family's C.L.T. Sandwich (Carrot, Lettuce & Tomato)

THE FAMILY'S C.L.T SANDWICH
(CARROT, LETTUCE & TOMATO)

SERVINGS: 2-3 SANDWICHES
PREP TIME: 15-30 MINS (Timing varies for marinating)
COOK TIME: 5-10 MINS

INGREDIENTS

3 medium carrots, peeled lengthwise with peeler

1 tsp smoked paprika

½ tsp cracked black pepper

1 tsp garlic powder

All-natural cracked sea salt (to taste)

3 tbsp all-natural maple syrup

1/3 cup all-natural soy sauce

1 tbsp extra virgin olive oil

Non-enriched, unbleached, all-natural bread

all-natural mayonnaise

2 cups romaine lettuce, chopped

1 small tomato, sliced

DIRECTIONS

1. Use peeler to cut carrots into thin slices.

2. In a bowl, add smoked paprika, black pepper, garlic powder, sea salt, maple syrup and soy sauce. Mix well. Add carrots and let sit and marinate for 10-20 minutes.

3. After marinating, place paper towel on top of a plate and place carrots on top of paper towel. Sprinkle cracked sea salt to tase. Let sit for 10 minutes to air dry.

4. Heat olive oil in skillet on medium-high heat.

5. Cook carrot bacon until preferred crispiness. Place on clean paper towel to soak up excess oil.

6. Assemble sandwich. Spread a thin layer of mayonnaise on both pieces of bread. Add carrot slices, then top with lettuce, then top with tomatoes.

7. Serve and savor!

NOTE: To take it up a notch, add our homemade pickles and homemade jalapeños.

"A recipe has no soul. You, as the cook, must bring soul to the recipe."

—Thomas Keller

Overnight Oats

OVERNIGHT OATS

SERVINGS: 1 MASON JAR
PREP TIME: 5 MINS
CHILL TIME: 8 HRS

INGREDIENTS

½ cup Whole grain rolled oats

½ cup + 2 tbsp all-natural plant-based milk (almond milk, oat milk, walnut milk, etc.)

½ tsp Chia seeds

1 tbsp all-natural light agave or pure maple syrup

1 tsp pure vanilla extract

fresh fruit, ex. blueberries, raspberries, strawberries,

peaches, bananas, pears, apples (optional, to your liking)

dried fruit, ex. raisins, cranberries, chopped dates (optional, to your liking)

nuts and seeds, ex. sliced almonds, chopped pecans, chopped walnuts, sunflower seeds (optional, to your liking)

spices, ex. cinnamon, turmeric, cardamom, ginger (optional, to your liking)

DIRECTIONS

1. Add oats, milk, chia seeds, agave or maple syrup and vanilla extract to a jar that has a tight, sealable lid (ex. mason jar). Stir all ingredients until combined.

2. Close lid tightly and let it soak in fridge overnight (approx. 8 hrs.).

3. When ready to eat, add your favorite toppings (ex. fresh fruit, dried fruit, nuts, seeds and spices) and mix. You can add more milk to reach your desired consistency.

4. Serve and savor!

"Success is to be measured not so much by the position that one has reached in life as by the obstacles which he has overcome."

—Booker T. Washington

RAW

Raw Coconut Curry Tranquility

RAW COCONUT CURRY TRANQUILITY

SERVINGS: 2
PREP TIME: 20 MINS
COOK TIME: N/A

INGREDIENTS

¼ orange baby bell pepper, thinly sliced

¼ red baby bell pepper, thinly sliced

½ cup fresh broccoli florets, chopped

1 tbsp scallions, chopped

1/3 cup cilantro, chopped

1 cup all-natural coconut cream

2 garlic cloves, minced

1 medium tomato, cut into big chunks

½ tsp fresh ginger, remove skin and minced

2 small carrots, cut into small-med chunks

1 tsp all-natural coarse salt

2 tsp curry powder

¼ tsp red pepper flakes (optional, to your liking)

2 tbsp fresh squeezed lemon juice

Spring water (to adjust consistency to your liking, if needed)

DIRECTIONS

1. Place bell peppers, broccoli, scallions and cilantro to the side.

2. Blend coconut cream, garlic, tomato, ginger, carrots, salt, curry powder, red pepper flakes, lemon juice and water for 1 minute or until well blended. Add spring water if needed.

3. Pour blended soup in bowl, top with the vegetables that you put to the side.

4. Serve and savor!

Vineyard Delight

VINEYARD DELIGHT

SERVINGS: 1
PREP TIME: 5 MINUTES
COOK TIME: N/A

INGREDIENTS

1 ripe avocado, peeled, pitted, cut into chunks

7-10 grape tomatoes, halved

All-natural cracked sea salt (to taste)

Cracked black pepper (to taste)

Chipotle powder (to taste)

¼ lemon, squeezed

1-2 tbsp cilantro, minced

DIRECTIONS

1. Place chunks of avocado on a plate with chunks spread apart.

2. Plate the grape tomatoes on top of the avocado.

3. Sprinkle lightly with salt, pepper and chipotle powder (to your liking).

4. Squeeze lemon over avocado and tomatoes.

5. Garnish with cilantro.

6. Serve and savor!

Summer Sunset Zucchini Salad

SUMMER SUNSET ZUCCHINI SALAD

SERVINGS: 4
PREP TIME: 10 MINS
COOK TIME: N/A

INGREDIENTS

5 small-medium zucchinis, sliced with peeler

1/3 cup fresh parsley, chopped

1/3 cup fresh cilantro, chopped

10-15 fresh basil leaves, chopped

6-8 fresh mint leaves, chopped

1/3 cup crushed pistachios

½ tsp all-natural cracked sea salt

½ tsp cracked black pepper

2 tbsp extra virgin olive oil

1 lemon, squeezed

DIRECTIONS

1. In a medium bowl, add zucchinis, parsley, cilantro, basil, mint, pistachios, salt, black pepper, olive oil and lemon juice. Mix all ingredients together until well combined.

2. Serve and savor!

"Change will not come if we wait for some other person or some other time. We are the ones we've been waiting for. We are the change that we seek."

—Barack Obama

SOUPS

Enchanted Enchilada Soup

ENCHANTED ENCHILADA SOUP

SERVINGS: 8
PREP TIME: 10 MINS
COOK TIME: 1 HR

INGREDIENTS

3 large chicken breasts (4-5 lbs.)

spring water (to boil chicken)

1-½ tbsp all-natural coarse salt

3 tsp garlic powder

3 tsp onion powder

1 tsp smoked paprika

¼ cup + 2 tbsp extra virgin olive oil

½ sweet onion, diced

5 garlic cloves, minced

½ cup Masa Harina (Instant Corn Masa)

2 cups all-natural coconut milk

32 oz all-natural chicken broth

14 oz all-natural black beans, drained and rinsed

14 oz all-natural pinto beans, drained and rinsed

2 cans all-natural corn (15.25 oz or 4 cups)

16 oz all-natural tomato sauce

2/3 cup all-natural salsa

2 tbsp chili powder

2 tsp cumin

1 lime, squeezed

2 tbsp fresh cilantro, chopped

Monterey Jack cheese (to your liking)

All-natural tortilla chips (optional, to your liking)

Avocado (optional, to your liking)

Green onion (optional, to your liking)

DIRECTIONS

1. In large saucepan, on high heat, add chicken and cover with spring water. Add ½ tbsp all-natural coarse salt, 1 tsp garlic powder, 1 tsp onion powder and 1 tsp smoked paprika. Bring to a boil.

2. Once chicken comes to a boil, reduce heat to medium and allow chicken to cook for 30 minutes.

3. Remove chicken from pot and allow to cool down. Set aside.

4. While the chicken is cooling down, in the large saucepan on medium to high heat, add ¼ cup + 2 tbsp of olive oil, onions and garlic. Allow to sauté for about 3 minutes.

5. Prepare a roux by stirring in the Masa Harina. Slowly pour in 2 cups of coconut milk. Cook while stirring constantly until mixture reaches a gentle boil. (Mixture will be thick!) Add chicken broth and stir well. Bring to a boil.

6. Add beans, corn, tomato sauce and salsa. Stir well. Reduce heat to low.

7. Add remaining 1 tbsp salt, 2 tsp of onion powder, 2 tsp of garlic powder, 2 tbsp of chili powder and 1 tsp of cumin. Stir in the spices.

8. Chicken breast should be cooled down by now. Shred chicken with a fork and add to saucepan. Cover and cook for about 20 minutes.

9. Add cilantro, squeezed lime and more salt to taste.

10. Serve in a bowl and top with Monterey Jack cheese. You can also top with avocado, green onions or tortilla strips.

11. Serve and savor!

"You're not obligated to win. You're obligated to keep trying to do the best you can every day."

—Marian Wright Edelman

Cozy Cabbage Soup

COZY CABBAGE SOUP

SERVINGS: 8-10
PREP TIME: 20 MINS
COOK TIME: 35 MINS

INGREDIENTS

6 tbsp extra virgin olive oil

1 medium red bell pepper, sliced and halved

1 green bell pepper, sliced and halved

1 small, sweet onion, sliced

3 medium carrots, diced

3 celery sticks, diced

5 garlic cloves, minced

2 fresh cobs of corn (use knife to cut off kernels)

1 sweet potato, cubed

2 cups all-natural diced tomatoes

62 oz all-natural vegetable broth

1 tbsp fresh rosemary, destemmed

1 tbsp fresh thyme, destemmed

1 tbsp all-natural coarse salt

½ tsp cracked black pepper

1 medium cabbage, chopped

1 tsp red pepper flakes (optional)

Parsley (optional)

Crystal's hot sauce, to taste

DIRECTIONS

1. In a dutch oven pot, on high heat, add 6 tbsp olive oil.

2. Add bell peppers, onions, carrots, celery and garlic. Stir. Cook for 10 minutes, stirring every 2 minutes.

3. Add corn, sweet potatoes, diced tomatoes, and broth. Add rosemary, thyme, salt, black pepper and red pepper flakes. Stir well.

4. Bring to a boil then add the cabbage. Cover pot. Cook for 10 minutes or until cabbage is soft with a little crunch.

5. Add hot sauce and stir. Add parsley.

6. Serve and savor!

Creamy Chicken Noodle Soup

CREAMY CHICKEN NOODLE SOUP

SERVINGS: 8
PREP TIME: 10 MINS
COOK TIME: 1 HR 15 MINS

INGREDIENTS

2 lbs. boneless skinless chicken breast, halved)

1-½ tbsp all-natural coarse salt

1 tbsp garlic powder

1 tbsp onion powder

4 bay leaves

¼ cup extra virgin olive oil

¼ small, sweet onion, diced

5 garlic cloves, minced

4 carrots, chopped

3 celery stalks, chopped

7 cups all-natural vegetable broth

½ tsp red pepper flakes

1 tbsp tarragon

4 cups fresh broccoli florets, chopped

¼ cup virgin unrefined coconut oil

1/3 cup unbleached, non-enriched all-purpose flour

1-½ cup all-natural coconut milk

1 cup all-natural cream of chicken soup

16 oz all-natural, non-enriched farfalle noodles

1 tsp cracked black pepper

DIRECTIONS

1. In a large pot, on high heat, bring chicken to a boil. Add ½ tbsp salt, ½ tbsp garlic powder, ½ tbsp onion powder and 4 bay leaves. Allow to boil until chicken is cooked through (about 30 minutes).

2. Remove chicken breasts from pot. Set aside to allow to cool.

3. In another large pot, on medium heat, add olive oil. Add onions, garlic, carrots and celery. Sauté until tender (about 10 minutes).

4. Increase heat to medium-high. Add vegetable broth, 1 tbsp salt, black pepper, ½ tsp red pepper flakes, ½ tbsp onion powder, ½ tbsp garlic powder and 1 tbsp tarragon. Stir well.

5. While that's heating up, you should now be able to shred the chicken with a fork. Add shredded chicken to the pot with the broth. Once boiling, reduce heat to low.

6. Add broccoli florets and stir.

7. In a small saucepan, on medium heat, add ¼ cup coconut oil. When oil is hot, add 1/3 cup of flour. Whisk for about 2 minutes. Slowly add in coconut milk. Continue to whisk to remove any lumps. Add cream of chicken soup. Whisk together. Remove from heat and add to pot with the chicken. Stir well.

8. Cook noodles according to directions listed on package and drain.

9. Add cooked noodles to pot with chicken and stir.

10. Serve and savor!

*"Tell me what you eat,
and I will tell you what you are."*

—Anthelme Brillat-Savarin

Tortellini Soup

TORTELLINI SOUP

SERVINGS: 7
PREP TIME: 10 MINS
COOK TIME: 35 MINS

INGREDIENTS

¼ cup extra virgin olive oil or virgin unrefined coconut oil

½ medium sweet or yellow onion, diced

4 garlic cloves, minced

3-4 medium tomatoes, diced

All-natural tomato basil sauce (24 oz) (preferably low sodium)

½ tbsp all-natural coarse salt (to taste)

½ tsp black pepper

½ tbsp garlic powder

1 tsp onion powder

½ tsp fresh rosemary, destemmed and minced

2 tsp fresh thyme, destemmed

1 tsp fresh basil, minced

½ tsp red pepper flakes (to taste)

½ lemon, squeezed

2 cartons of all-natural vegetable broth (32 oz)

1 bag all-natural, non-enriched tortellini pasta (12 oz)

2 cups all-natural coconut milk

2 handfuls of Baby spinach

Cilantro, chopped (optional, to taste)

DIRECTIONS

1. In a large pot, on medium-high heat, add olive oil or coconut oil.

2. Once oil is hot, add onions and garlic. Cook for about 3 minutes, stirring every minute.

3. Add tomatoes. Stir well. When the tomatoes begin to simmer, add basil sauce, salt, black pepper, garlic powder, onion powder, rosemary, thyme, basil, and red pepper. Allow everything to cook for about 10 minutes while stirring every 3 minutes.

43

4. Add tomato sauce and stir. Reduce heat to medium. Cover and cook for 5 minutes while stirring every couple of minutes.

5. Add broth. Increase heat to high. Bring to a rapid boil. Add the lemon juice. Add tortellini pasta. Cook according to directions on pack.

6. Remove from heat. Shake can of coconut milk since contents may be separated. If coconut milk is still not mixed well, pour into a large cup and whisk until combined. Add coconut milk. Stir well.

7. Add spinach and cilantro.

8. Serve and savor!

*"Good food is very often,
even most often,
simple food."*

—Anthony Bourdain

Kale & Farro Stew

KALE & FARRO STEW

SERVINGS: 6-8
PREP TIME: 15 MINS
COOK TIME: 45 MINS

INGREDIENTS

2 tbsp extra virgin olive oil

2 medium carrots, diced

1 small, sweet onion, diced

5 garlic cloves, minced

2 tbsp fresh lemon grass, minced

2 celery sticks, chopped

5 cups all-natural vegetable broth

28 oz all-natural San Marzano tomatoes

1 cup all-natural, non-enriched farro

½ tbsp oregano

2 bay leaves

1 tbsp all-natural salt (to taste)

4 cups kale (chopped)

14 oz all-natural cannellini beans, drained and rinsed

½ lemon, squeezed

DIRECTIONS

1. Heat olive oil in a large pot over medium-high heat.

2. Add carrots, onion, garlic, lemon grass and celery. Sauté for about 4 minutes.

3. Add vegetable broth, tomatoes, farro, oregano, bay leaves and salt. Stir well and bring to a boil.

4. Reduce heat to medium. Cover with lid and simmer for 20 minutes.

5. Add kale. Stir and cook for about 15 minutes longer or until farro is tender.

6. Remove bay leaves and add cannellini beans. Stir well.

7. Stir in lemon juice and add more broth or spring water if soup is too thick.

8. Serve and savor!

"Eating healthy food fills your body with energy and nutrients. Imagine your cells smiling back at you and saying: 'Thank you!'"

—Karen Salmansohn

RICE & QUINOA

Granny's Pigeon Peas & Rice

GRANNY'S PIGEON PEAS & RICE

SERVINGS: 6-8
PREP TIME: 15 MINS
COOK TIME: 30 MINS

INGREDIENTS

2 15.5 oz. cans dry pigeon peas

½ tbsp + 1 tsp all-natural coarse salt

2 tbsp oregano

½ tbsp basil

½ tsp black pepper

½ tsp thyme

½ tsp cumin

½ tbsp garlic powder

½ tbsp onion powder

1-½ tbsp parsley

3 tbsp virgin unrefined coconut oil

1 small sweet onion (diced)

1 medium green bell pepper (diced)

5 cups all-natural chicken or vegetable broth

½ cup all-natural ketchup

4 cups non-enriched jasmine rice

DIRECTIONS

1. In a medium pot, on high heat, bring pigeon peas to a boil. Once boiling, reduce heat to medium-low and cook for 20 minutes. Add spring water if needed.

2. While peas are cooking, in a small bowl, combine salt, oregano, basil, black pepper, thyme, cumin, garlic powder, onion powder and parsley. Set aside.

3. In a large pot, on medium-high heat, add coconut oil.

4. Once oil is hot, add onions and bell peppers. Stir and sauté for about 5 minutes.

5. Pigeon peas should be done cooking now. Drain peas and add to pot with onions and bell peppers. Increase heat to high.

6. Add broth, ketchup and seasonings. Stir well.

7. Once broth begins to boil, add rice and stir to mix well. Reduce heat to low. Cover with lid and cook for about 20 minutes. Stir rice occasionally (about every 3 minutes) to prevent sticking.

8. When rice is done cooking, remove from heat and let sit for 10 minutes.

9. Fluff up rice with a fork.

10. Serve and savor!

"Eating well is a form of self-respect."

—Unknown

Sunlit Quinoa Salad

SUNLIT QUINOA SALAD

SERVINGS: 8-10
PREP TIME: 30 MINS
COOK TIME: VARIES BASED ON COOKING INSTRUCTIONS FOR QUINOA. CHECK YOUR PACK.

INGREDIENTS

1 cup cooked quinoa

2 cobs of corn, uncooked, strip kernels

2-3 avocados, peeled, pitted and sliced

¼ cup red onion, thinly sliced

½ cup cilantro, minced

1 tbsp extra virgin olive oil

1-½ cup grape tomatoes, cut into fourths

3 garlic cloves, minced

½ tsp cracked sea salt

½ tsp cracked black pepper

½ lemon, squeezed

DIRECTIONS

1. Cook quinoa according to directions on the pack.

2. While quinoa is cooking, add corn, avocados, onion, cilantro, olive oil, grape tomatoes, minced garlic cloves, salt, and black pepper to a salad bowl and mix well.

3. Once quinoa is done cooking, place in the fridge to cool down. Once quinoa is cooled, add to salad bowl.

4. Squeeze lemon juice in salad bowl and mix all contents thoroughly.

5. Serve and savor!

Seasoned Rice

SEASONED RICE

SERVINGS: 6-8
PREP TIME: 5 MINS
COOK TIME: 13 MINS

INGREDIENTS

2 cups non-enriched Jasmine rice

2 tbsp extra virgin olive oil

2-½ cups spring water or all-natural chicken broth

1 tsp garlic powder

1 tsp onion powder

1 tsp paprika

½ tsp ground thyme

1 tsp all-natural coarse salt

½ tsp cracked black pepper

2 tbsp parsley, for garnish

DIRECTIONS

1. In a medium sized pot, add the olive oil. Heat the olive oil for about 1 minute, remove from heat and add rice. Stir rice until the olive oil is all over rice.

2. Add water or chicken broth.

3. Mix the garlic powder, onion powder, paprika, thyme, salt, and black pepper. Stir gently.

4. Place pot back on high heat and bring to a boil. Reduce heat to low (for strong stoves) and cover pot with a tightly covered lid.

5. Cook for 13 minutes. DO NOT LIFT LID.

6. Remove from heat. Let stand for 10 minutes with lid on, undisturbed.

7. Fluff rice with fork. Add salt and pepper to tase, if needed.

8. Garnish with parsley.

9. Serve and savor!

Grandma Delois' Perlo Rice (without Meat)

GRANDMA DELOIS' PERLO RICE (WITHOUT MEAT)

SERVINGS: 6-7
PREP TIME: 10 MINS
COOK TIME: 30 MINS

INGREDIENTS

3 cups non-enriched Jasmine rice

2 tbsp extra virgin olive oil

½ tbsp + 1 tsp all-natural coarse salt

Spring water

1 tbsp virgin unrefined coconut oil

1 small or medium green bell pepper, diced

1-½ tsp cracked black pepper

1 sweet or yellow onion, diced

1-½ cracked black pepper

DIRECTIONS

1. In a large saucepan, on high heat, add 1 tbsp olive oil, 3 cups of rice and ½ tbsp salt. Mix until oil is all over the rice. Use spring water for water measurement on the pack of rice. Cook rice as directed on the pack.

2. In a medium non-stick skillet, on high heat, immediately add 1 tbsp coconut oil and 1 tbsp olive oil. As soon as coconut oil melts, add bell peppers and onions to skillet. Add 1 tsp salt and 1-½ tsp cracked black pepper. Mix well.

3. When you notice a slight browning of sauteed vegetables, reduce heat to medium-high. Mix constantly to prevent burning. Sautee vegetables until you see a little browning (about 5-7 minutes). Remove from heat until rice is done cooking.

4. Once rice is done cooking, add sauteed vegetables to the pot of rice. Combine well until there are no more white chunks of rice.

5. Add more salt and pepper to taste.

6. Serve and savor!

Grandma Delois' Perlo Rice (with Chicken)

GRANDMA DELOIS' PERLO RICE (WITH CHICKEN)

SERVINGS: 6-8
PREP TIME: 5 MINS
COOK TIME: 1 HR

INGREDIENTS

3 lbs. boneless, skinless chicken thighs

9 cups spring water

1-½ tbsp all-natural coarse salt

1-½ tbsp cracked black pepper

1 sweet or yellow onion, sliced and halved

1 medium green bell pepper, sliced and halved

2 tbsp extra virgin olive oil

3 cups non-enriched Jasmine rice

1 tbsp virgin unrefined coconut oil

DIRECTIONS

1. In a large pot, on high heat, add chicken, water, 1 tbsp salt, 1 tbsp black pepper, onions, and bell pepper. Bring to a boil. Allow chicken to boil until chicken is cooked through (roughly 35 minutes).

2. Drain the chicken, onions and bell peppers through a strainer and catch the chicken broth in a large bowl. Set aside.

3. In the same pot, on medium-high heat, add 1 tbsp olive oil. Add jasmine rice and stir gently until oil is all over rice.

4. Stir the broth that was set aside and measure according to rice pack and add to pot of rice. Cook according to directions on pack.

5. While the rice is cooking, remove chicken from strainer and cut into bite-sized chunks. Set aside.

6. Remove onions and bell peppers from strainer and dice into smaller pieces. Set aside.

7. In a large non-stick skillet, on medium-high heat, add 1 tbsp coconut oil and 1 tbsp olive oil. Once oil is hot, add chicken, onions and bell peppers and cook for 5 minutes, stirring every few minutes.

8. Once rice is done cooking, add chicken, onions and bell peppers to pot of rice. Add ½ tbsp salt and ½ tbsp black pepper and stir gently until mixed through. (Add salt and pepper to taste)

9. Serve and savor!

<u>PASTA</u>

Soulful Beef Stroganoff

SOULFUL BEEF STROGANOFF

SERVINGS: 5-6
PREP TIME: 10 MINS
COOK TIME: 25 MINS

INGREDIENTS

1-½ lbs. sirloin, ribeye or top round thin sliced steak (cut strips about ½ in. wide and 2 in. long)

1-½ tsp all-natural coarse salt

½ tsp cracked black pepper

1 tsp garlic powder

1 tsp onion powder

2 tsp fresh thyme, destemmed and minced

½ tsp mustard powder

4 tbsp extra virgin olive oil

½ small, sweet onion, diced

5 garlic cloves, minced

3 tbsp unbleached non-enriched all-purpose flour

2 cups all-natural beef broth

1-½ tbsp Worcestershire sauce

2 tsp all-natural Dijon mustard

1 tsp gravy master

1 cup all-natural coconut milk

2 cups baby spinach, roughly chopped

16 oz all-natural non-enriched egg noodles

Spring water (to cook egg noodles)

parsley (optional, for garnish)

DIRECTIONS

1. In a medium bowl, add sliced steak and salt, black pepper, garlic powder, onion powder, thyme, and mustard powder. Mix together well until spices evenly cover the steak.

2. In a large non-stick skillet, heat olive oil on medium-high heat.

3. Once the oil gets hot, add onions and garlic. Allow to sauté for about 3 minutes, stirring every minute.

4. Add seasoned steak to the skillet. Stir well until onions, garlic and oil is covering all of the steak.

5. Allow steak to cook for about 15 minutes, stirring every 4-5 minutes.

6. While steak is cooking, prepare the broth. In a large cup, add the flour. In the same cup, add the broth while SIMULTANEOUSLY whisking to prevent flour from caking. Add Worcestershire sauce, Dijon mustard and gravy master to the cup. Mix well.

7. Once steak is cooked through and some browning forms at the bottom of the skillet, pour broth into skillet and stir. Once sauce begins to thicken, reduce heat to low and add coconut milk and spinach. Stir well. Add salt to taste.

8. In a medium saucepan, boil egg noodles with spring water to your desired tenderness (refer to directions on pack).

9. Serve beef over egg noodles. Garnish with parsley. Serve and savor!

*"Take care of your body.
It's the only place you have to live."*

—Jim Rohn

Cajun Naturalite Veggie Alfredo

CAJUN NATURALITE VEGGIE ALFREDO

SERVINGS: 6
PREP TIME: 20 MINS
COOK TIME: 35 MINS

INGREDIENTS

2 heads of broccoli, cut into florets (optional: remove hard skin from stems and dice stems)

1 1/8 cup extra virgin olive oil

2-½ tsp all-natural coarse salt

1 tsp cracked black pepper

¾ tsp red pepper flakes

½ tsp garlic powder

¼ lime, squeezed

16 oz. all-natural, non-enriched Fettuccini pasta

1 cup red onion, diced

1 cup orange or yellow bell pepper, diced

7 garlic cloves, smashed and minced

1 tsp onion powder

1 tsp French herb blend or ½ tsp thyme and ½ tsp oregano

3 cups kale, rough chopped

½ tsp smoked paprika

½ tsp cayenne pepper

1 cup grape tomatoes, diced

1-½ tbsp corn starch

27.32 oz. all-natural coconut milk (two 13.66 oz. cans)

DIRECTIONS

1. Preheat oven to 400°F.

2. Add broccoli florets and stems to a bag. Add ¼ cup of olive oil, 1 tsp all-natural coarse salt, ½ tsp black pepper, ½ tsp red pepper flakes, ½ tsp garlic powder and squeeze lime juice to bag. Close bag tightly and mix all ingredients around until well combined.

3. In a baking dish, spread broccoli out and be sure to not over-crowd. Set aside.

4. Cook fettuccine according to directions on pack. Strain, drizzle a little olive oil over pasta to prevent sticking and set aside.

5. In a large saucepan, on medium-high heat, add ¼ cup olive oil. Once oil is hot, add onions and bell peppers. Stir and cook for about 1 minute. Add garlic, 1-½ tsp salt, ½ tsp black pepper, ¼ tsp red pepper flakes, 1 tsp onion powder and 1 tsp French blend herbs. Mix well and cook for another minute, then add kale. Stir and add ½ tsp smoked paprika and ½ tsp cayenne pepper. Stir and cook for about 5 minutes.

6. Add grape tomatoes. Stir and cook for 2 minutes. Remove from heat and transfer veggie mix to a bowl.

7. In the same saucepan, on medium heat, add 1/8 cup of olive oil and 1-½ tbsp of cornstarch and whisk into a rue. Let cook for about 1 minute until rue begins to thicken. Slowly, add coconut milk and stir well. Add cooked veggies back to saucepan. Stir and cook for about 5 minutes. When sauce begins to simmer, reduce heat to medium-low.

8. While sauce is cooking, bake the broccoli in the oven for about 6 minutes.

9. Once the sauce is done cooking, add the cooked fettuccini to the saucepan and stir well. Add cooked broccoli and gently stir together.

10. Serve and savor!

NOTE: Pairs well topped with our Sauteed Royal Trumpet Mushrooms.

*"The food you eat can be either
the safest and most powerful form of
medicine or the slowest form of poison."*

—Ann Wigmore

Tempting Tuna Salad (No Egg, No Tuna)

Tempting Tuna Salad

72

TEMPTING TUNA SALAD

SERVINGS: 8-10
PREP TIME: 15 MINS
COOK TIME: 9-12 MINS

INGREDIENTS

16 oz all-natural non-enriched macaroni elbows

½ red bell pepper, finely chopped

½ green bell pepper, finely chopped

½ red onion, finely chopped

4 large brown eggs, boiled, peeled and chopped (optional)

2 5 oz. cans all-natural Albacore Tuna (in water) (optional)

1 cup all-natural relish or our Homemade Pickle recipe, finely chopped

1 cup all-natural mayonnaise

2 tbsp all-natural mustard

1 tsp all-natural cracked sea salt

1 tsp cracked black pepper

1 tbsp raw cane sugar

DIRECTIONS

1. Cook elbows as directed on pack. Drain and allow to cool down completely before mixing.

2. If using eggs in recipe, boil until cooked through (usually 9-12 minutes).

3. In a large mixing bowl, add bell peppers, onion, eggs (optional), tuna (optional), relish, mayonnaise, mustard, salt, black pepper, and sugar. Mix well.

4. Refrigerate for at least 1 hour before serving.

5. Serve and savor!

NOTE: If you are eating the tuna salad as leftovers and it is dry, add a little mayonnaise until you reach your desired consistency. Also, for the relish, you can use our Homemade Pickle recipe.

This can also be made meatless. Use the same recipe, minus the tuna and eggs.

VEGETABLES

Pan Seared Brussel Sprouts

PAN SEARED BRUSSEL SPROUTS

SERVINGS: 4-6
PREP TIME: 5 MINS
COOK TIME: 15 MINS

INGREDIENTS

16 oz brussels sprouts, halved

5 tbsp extra virgin olive oil

¼ tsp garlic powder

1 tsp all-natural cracked sea salt
(adjust to taste)

½ tsp cracked black pepper

¼ tsp onion powder

2 garlic cloves, minced

1/8 lemon, squeezed

DIRECTIONS

1. Cut off the stems of the sprouts. Remove any dead leaves. Cut in half and rinse dirt from sprouts.

2. In a bowl, mix Brussel sprouts, 1 tbsp of olive oil, garlic powder, salt, pepper, onion powder and garlic until evenly coated.

3. Heat large nonstick skillet or cast-iron skillet on medium heat. Pour 4 tbsp of olive oil in skillet.

4. Add brussel sprouts to skillet with flat surface facing down. Cook for about 5 to 10 minutes or until browned. Flip over and cook additional 5 minutes or until browned.

5. Squeeze lemon over sprouts and gently stir.

6. Serve and savor!

Crispy Baked Asparagus

CRISPY BAKED ASPARAGUS

SERVINGS: 4-5
PREP TIME: 5 MINS
COOK TIME: 20 MINS

INGREDIENTS

24 oz asparagus

1-½ tsp extra virgin olive oil

1-½ tsp all-natural coarse salt

½ tsp cracked black pepper

1 tsp garlic powder

½ tsp onion powder

DIRECTIONS

1. Turn oven on to Broil.

2. Trim off about 1 inch of the bottom of asparagus.

3. Place asparagus on a large cookie sheet that has small, elevated edges or a baking pan.

4. Pour olive oil over asparagus. Sprinkle salt, black pepper, garlic powder and onion powder over the asparagus.

5. Gently mix with hands until evenly coated with spices and oil. Spread the asparagus out evenly to allow even flow of cooking.

6. Place in the oven on the 2nd from top rack and broil for 15 minutes.

7. Remove from oven. Gently mix asparagus around. Drain juices if there are any. Broil for another 5 minutes.

8. Immediately serve while hot and savor!

Southern Style Smoked Green Beans

SOUTHERN STYLE SMOKED GREEN BEANS

SERVINGS: 6-8
PREP TIME: 15 MINS
COOK TIME: 40 MINS

INGREDIENTS

1-½ cups smoked turkey drumstick meat (remove tough skin, cut meat off bone and chopped)

½ cup extra virgin olive oil

5 garlic cloves, smashed and minced

½ medium sweet onion, sliced

2 lbs. of fresh green beans, trimmed ends (If green bean is too long, cut in half)

6-8 cups of spring water

1 tsp garlic powder

2 tbsp all-natural coarse salt

½ tbsp smoked paprika

DIRECTIONS

1. In large saucepan, on medium-high heat, add the olive oil.

2. Once the oil is hot, add the turkey meat, garlic, and onions.

3. Cook for about 5 minutes, stirring every 2 minutes.

4. Add green beans and spring water. (Just enough water to cover the green beans). Add garlic powder, salt and paprika. Stir well. Cover with lid and turn heat on high.

5. Once the green beans begin to boil, reduce heat to medium-low. Cook for a remaining 35 minutes.

6. **OPTIONAL:** Drain most of the juice.

7. Serve and savor!

Smoked Kale Greens

SMOKED KALE GREENS

SERVINGS: 5-6
PREP TIME: 10 MINS
COOK TIME: 30 MINS

INGREDIENTS

¼ cup extra virgin olive oil

1 cup smoked turkey legs or wings, meat cut from bone and roughly chopped

1 small, sweet onion, thinly sliced

1 small red pepper, thinly sliced then halved

2 bundles of kale, destemmed and roughly chopped

32 oz. all-natural vegetable broth

1 tsp oregano

½ tbsp all-natural coarse salt

1-½ tbsp + 1 tsp garlic powder

1 tsp red pepper flakes (to taste)

2 tbsp distilled white vinegar

DIRECTIONS

1. In a large saucepan, on medium-high heat, add olive oil. Once oil is hot, add smoked turkey. Let turkey cook for about 5 minutes while stirring every minute or so to not stick to bottom.

2. Add in onions and bell peppers. Stir really well and cook for about 5 minutes while stirring about every 2 minutes.

3. Add half of the chopped kale to the saucepan. Add ½ of vegetable broth and stir well until you see kale turning darker green and shrinking.

4. Add remaining kale and rest of broth to pot. Stir again until well combined. Increase heat to high heat.

5. Once kale beings to boil, reduce heat to medium-low. Add the oregano, salt, garlic powder, red pepper flakes and vinegar. Stir well. Cover pot. Let cook for about 20 minutes, stirring every 5 minutes.

6. Serve and savor!

Veggie Stuffed Bell Peppers

VEGGIE STUFFED BELL PEPPERS

SERVINGS: 8
PREP TIME: 15 MINS
COOK TIME: 1-½ HR

INGREDIENTS

6 large bell peppers of any color (halved and deseeded)

2 tbsp extra virgin olive oil

½ small, sweet onion, diced

4 garlic cloves, minced

5 cups kale, chopped

4-½ cups all-natural vegetable broth or spring water

2 cups bulgur wheat

3 tsp all-natural coarse salt

1 15 oz. can all-natural kernel corn

1 15 oz. can all-natural black beans

3 tsp cumin powder

2 tsp chili powder

2 tsp thyme

2 tsp garlic powder

1 cup all-natural salsa

8 oz block pepper jack cheese, shredded

2 tbsp parsley

DIRECTIONS

1. Heat oven to 350 degrees Fahrenheit. Place bell peppers on a nonstick baking dish and bake for 15-20 minutes (depending on thickness of peppers). Once the peppers are done baking, remove excess water from peppers and set aside.

2. In a large saucepan, on medium-high heat, add 3 tbsp olive oil, onions and minced garlic. Cook for about 3 minutes, stirring about every minute.

3. Add kale to saucepan. Mix well to combine. Let cook down for 5 minutes while stirring every minute.

4. Add broth or water to saucepan. Place on high heat and bring to a boil. Add bulgur wheat and salt. Stir and decrease heat to low. Cover and cook for 30 minutes.

5. Drain corn and add corn and black beans to another medium pot. Add cumin, chili, thyme, garlic powder and salsa. Mix well. Cook on medium-high heat until simmering.

6. Once the bulgur wheat is done cooking, add corn and bean mix to bulgur wheat and stir well.

7. Stuff peppers with bulgur wheat mixture then top with cheese.

8. Bake for 15 minutes. Broil for 3 minutes or until cheese is slightly browned. Time will vary.

9. Remove peppers from oven and garnish with parsley.

10. Serve and savor!

NOTE: Paired well with our Garlic Cilantro Sauce drizzled over top of baked bell peppers.

*"Your diet is a bank account.
Good food choices are good investments."*

—Bethenny Frankel

Sauteed Royal Trumpet Mushrooms

SAUTEED ROYAL TRUMPET MUSHROOMS

SERVINGS: 3-4 MINS
PREP TIME: 5 MINS
COOK TIME: 8 MINS

INGREDIENTS

¼ cup + 1 tbsp extra virgin olive oil or grapeseed oil

6 oz. royal trumpet mushrooms, sliced

1 tsp all-natural coarse salt

½ tsp cracked black pepper

1 tsp smoked paprika

1 tsp French blend herbs

½ tsp garlic powder

¼ lemon, squeezed

DIRECTIONS

1. Add mushrooms, salt, black pepper, smoked paprika, French blend herbs, garlic powder, lemon juice and ¼ cup olive oil or grapeseed oil to a clean bag or zip lock bag. Close the bag and mix all ingredients around until well combined.

2. In a large nonstick skillet or cast-iron skillet, on medium-high heat, add 1 tbsp olive oil or grapeseed oil.

3. Once oil is hot, add mushrooms to skillet. Stir and cook for about 8 minutes while stirring every couple of minutes.

4. Remove from heat.

5. Serve and savor!

Fried Cauliflower Nuggets

FRIED CAULIFLOWER NUGGETS

SERVINGS: 4-6
PREP TIME: 10 MINS
COOK TIME: 20 MINS

INGREDIENTS

1 cup non-enriched, unbleached, all-purpose flour

1 tsp baking powder

½ cup cornstarch

1 tbsp all-natural coarse salt

1 cup spring water

1 tbsp all-natural hot sauce

2 cups all-natural, non-enriched plain panko breadcrumbs

1 tbsp Italian seasoning or French herb blend

½ tbsp garlic powder

½ tbsp onion powder

½ tbsp smoked paprika

½ tbsp cayenne pepper

1 head of cauliflower, cut into small chunks

24 oz bottle grapeseed oil (or any other natural oil good for frying)

DIRECTIONS

1. In a medium bowl, mix flour, baking powder, cornstarch, and ½ tbsp salt. Add water and hot sauce. Mix well until batter is smooth.

2. In a separate medium bowl, add breadcrumbs, French herb blend, garlic powder, onion powder, paprika, and cayenne pepper. Make sure to mix well.

3. Dip cauliflower pieces in batter and coat evenly. Shake off any excess batter.

4. Roll the cauliflower chunks in breadcrumbs until coated thoroughly.

5. In medium frying pan, on medium heat, add oil.

91

6. Once the oil is heated, start adding cauliflower chunks to pan in batches. Once bottom side is golden brown, flip to the other side. Fry that side until golden brown.

7. Drain the oil off of cauliflower on paper towels.

8. Serve and savor!

NOTE: Dip them in our Super Secret Special Sauce!

"When diet is wrong, medicine is of no use.
When diet is correct, medicine is of no need."

—Ayurvedic Proverb

Rainbow Vegetable Medley

RAINBOW VEGETABLE MEDLEY

SERVINGS: 6-8
PREP TIME: 15 MINS
COOK TIME: 10 MINS

INGREDIENTS

2 tbsp grapeseed oil

3 medium carrots, sliced

3-4 cups fresh green beans, snipped

2 tsp all-natural coarse salt

½ tsp cracked black pepper

½ medium red onion, sliced

½ red bell pepper, sliced and halved

½ yellow bell pepper, sliced and halved

3-5 garlic cloves, minced

½ tsp red pepper flakes

½ tsp paprika

½ tsp onion powder

1 tbsp spring water

½ lime, squeezed

1 tsp extra virgin olive oil

1 tbsp cilantro, chopped (for garnish)

DIRECTIONS

1. In a non-stick skillet or cast-iron skillet on medium-high heat, add 2 tbsp grapeseed oil. Once oil is hot, add carrots, green beans, salt and pepper.

2. Allow to cook for 5 minutes while stirring continually.

3. Add onions, bell peppers, garlic, red pepper flakes, paprika, and onion powder and cook for 2 minutes. Mix thoroughly.

4. Reduce heat to medium and add spring water. Mix thoroughly and cook for 3 minutes while stirring continuously.

5. Remove from heat and squeeze lime juice. Mix thoroughly.

6. Right before plating, add 1 tsp olive oil and mix well.

7. Garnish with cilantro. Serve and savor!

"Health requires healthy food."

—Roger Williams

POTATOES

Crispy Baked Potato Wedges

CRISPY BAKED POTATO WEDGES

SERVINGS: 5
PREP TIME: 15 MINS
COOK TIME: 30-40 MINS

INGREDIENTS

6-8 russet potatoes, cut into wedges

Spring water (to boil potatoes)

4 tbsp extra virgin olive oil

2 tbsp all-natural coarse salt

2 tbsp smoked paprika

1-½ tbsp garlic powder

1-½ tbsp onion powder

½ tsp cracked black pepper

DIRECTIONS

1. Preheat oven to 450 degrees Fahrenheit. Cover the baking sheet with parchment paper or grease the baking sheet.

2. Cut potatoes in 8 wedges for each potato. (Try and make all wedges the same size to ensure all are cooking at the same rate).

3. On high heat, in a large pot, add potato wedges and cover the wedges with spring water. As soon as the wedges begin to boil, drain them and set aside to allow to cool down.

4. In a small bowl, add salt, smoked paprika, garlic powder, onion powder and black pepper and mix well. Set aside.

5. In a large bowl, add wedges and olive oil. Toss to coat.

6. Gently sprinkle the seasoning mixture over the wedges and toss to coat until they are evenly seasoned.

7. Place seasoned wedges on baking sheet in a single layer. (Be sure to not have the wedges touching).

8. Bake in the preheated oven for 15-20 minutes or until golden brown on the bottom.

9. Once they're golden brown on one side, flip the wedges over and cook on the other side for another 15-20 minutes or until golden brown. Ensure wedges are tender enough to puncture with a fork.

10. Remove from oven. Serve and savor!

TIP: Best paired with our Family's Special French Fry Sauce

*"Our bodies are our gardens—
our wills are our gardeners."*

—William Shakespeare

Potato Salad (No Egg)

POTATO SALAD (NO EGG)

SERVINGS: 10
PREP TIME: 20 MINS
COOK TIME: 20 MINS

INGREDIENTS

4 lbs. russet potatoes (cut into chunks)

1 tbsp all-natural coarse salt

1 cup all-natural mayonnaise

2 tbsp all-natural mustard

½ cup celery, minced)

1-½ cup all-natural relish or our Homemade Pickle recipe, minced

1 cup red bell pepper, minced

½ cup purple cabbage, minced

½ cup sweet onion, minced

1 tsp cracked black pepper

1 tsp paprika

1-½ tbsp raw cane sugar

DIRECTIONS

1. In a large saucepan, on high heat, bring diced potatoes to a boil. Add salt. Boil for about 13 minutes or until tender.

2. Drain potatoes and allow to cool.

3. In a large bowl, add potatoes, mayo, mustard, celery, relish (or our homemade pickle recipe, minced), bell pepper, purple cabbage, onion, pepper, paprika and sugar.

4. Gently mix ingredients together. (DO NOT SQUISH POTATOES)

5. Refrigerate for at least an hour.

6. Serve and savor!

Not Your Typical Au Gratin Potatoes

NOT YOUR TYPICAL
AU GRATIN POTATOES

SERVINGS: 6
PREP TIME: 10 MINS
COOK TIME: 30 MINS

INGREDIENTS

5-6 medium gold or yellow potatoes, thinly sliced

½ sweet onion, sliced

1 tbsp all-natural coarse salt

1 tsp cracked black pepper

2 tsp + 3 tbsp extra virgin olive oil

3 tbsp unbleached non-enriched all-purpose flour

13.66 oz all-natural coconut milk

½ tsp garlic powder

½ tsp onion powder

½ tbsp mustard powder

½ tbsp smoked paprika

½ tbsp ground turmeric

¼ cup all-natural vegetable broth or spring water

DIRECTIONS

1. Preheat oven to 400 degrees Fahrenheit.

2. Rinse potatoes off in large bowl. Add onions, ½ tbsp salt, 1 tsp black pepper and 2 tsp olive oil. Mix well.

3. In medium saucepan, on medium-high heat, add 3 tbsp olive oil. Once the oil is hot, reduce the heat to medium and add flour while whisking continuously.

4. After about 1 minute, slowly add coconut milk and vegetable broth or spring water while whisking. Add ½ tbsp salt, ½ tsp garlic powder, ½ tsp onion powder, ½ tbsp mustard powder, ½ tbsp smoked paprika and ½ tbsp ground turmeric. Stir well and remove from heat once the liquid begins to thicken.

5. Add potatoes in layers to a glass baking pan. Then slowly pour liquid mixture over potatoes. Cover with foil. Place baking dish on bottom shelf in the oven and bake for 15 minutes.

6. Remove foil and bake for another 15 minutes.

7. Serve and savor!

"Those who think they have no time for healthy eating will sooner or later have to find time for illness."

—Edward Stanley

Creamy Ranch Mashed Potatoes

CREAMY RANCH MASHED POTATOES

SERVINGS: 6-8
PREP TIME: 5 MINS
COOK TIME: 15 MINS

INGREDIENTS

3 lbs. Russet potatoes, cut into medium-sized chunks (leave skin on)

Spring water

½ tbsp all-natural cracked sea salt

1 cup all-natural ranch dressing or our Homemade Ranch Dressing recipe)

½ cup all-natural coconut milk

Parsley (for garnish)

DIRECTIONS

1. In a large pot, on high heat, add potatoes and cover potatoes with water. Bring to a boil and let boil for about 15 minutes or until potatoes are tender.

2. Drain water from pot. Remove from heat. Add salt, ranch dressing and coconut milk.

3. Smash with a fork or a potato masher until you reach desired consistency.

4. Garnish with parsley.

5. Serve and savor!

NOTE: For the ranch dressing, you can use our Homemade Ranch Dressing recipe.

Roasted Seasoned Potatoes

ROASTED SEASONED POTATOES

SERVINGS: 2-3
PREP TIME: 5 MINS
COOK TIME: 20 MINS

INGREDIENTS

16 oz baby potatoes, halved

1-½ tbsp extra virgin olive oil

1 tsp all-natural cracked sea salt

½ tsp cracked black pepper

1 tsp smoked paprika

½ tsp onion powder

½ tsp garlic powder

½ tsp oregano

½ tsp basil

½ tsp turmeric

virgin unrefined coconut oil (for greasing baking pan)

DIRECTIONS

1. Preheat oven to 400 degrees Fahrenheit.

2. After washing potatoes, make sure to pack dry.

3. Add potatoes and olive oil, salt, black pepper, smoked paprika, onion powder, garlic powder, oregano, basil and turmeric to a bag.

4. Shake bag around to mix all ingredients thoroughly.

5. Grease baking pan with coconut oil to prevent sticking.

6. Add potatoes to baking pan, face down and bake for 20 minutes on center rack undisturbed.

7. Remove from oven.

8. Serve and savor.

"Life matters, so let's eat like it!"

—Jabez el Israel

MEATS

Miami Bliss Blackened Salmon

MIAMI BLISS BLACKENED SALMON

SERVINGS: 7
PREP TIME: 15 MINS
COOK TIME: 20 MINS

INGREDIENTS

1 slab of salmon (3 lbs.)

2 tbsp smoked paprika

2 tsp light or dark brown sugar

1-½ tsp garlic powder

1-½ tsp onion powder

2 tsp all-natural coarse salt

1 tsp cayenne pepper

1 tsp oregano

1 tsp ground thyme

1-½ tbsp virgin unrefined coconut oil, melted

2 tbsp extra virgin olive oil

1 lemon, squeezed

DIRECTIONS

1. Clean salmon and pat dry. Cut into 2-3-inch-wide slabs.

2. In a small bowl, add the paprika, sugar, garlic powder, onion powder, salt, cayenne pepper, oregano, and thyme and mix well.

3. Brush the melted coconut oil over the meat side of the salmon. Sprinkle the seasoning mixture slowly and evenly with your fingers. Be sure to season the sides of the fillets as well.

4. Heat a large cast iron skillet or a large non-stick skillet on medium heat.

5. Add olive oil. Once the skillet is hot, slowly add the salmon fillets with the meat side down and cook for 5-10 minutes. (Timing may vary)

6. After about 5 minutes, carefully peak underneath to see if the salmon is blackened. Carefully flip the fillets over to have the skin side down.

7. Cook on the skin side for about 10 minutes or until the skin is crispy and the salmon is cooked through.

8. Remove from the heat and squeeze lemon over salmon.

9. Serve and savor!

"Every time you eat or drink, you are either feeding disease or fighting it."

—Heather Morgan

Crispy Crafted Beer Battered Fish

CRISPY CRAFTED BEER BATTERED FISH

SERVINGS: 7
PREP TIME: 15 MINS
COOK TIME: 25 MINS

INGREDIENTS

3 lbs. white fish like Cod or Grouper (cut into rectangular pieces about 2 in. wide and 3 in. long)

4-½ tsp all-natural coarse salt

1 tsp cracked black pepper

2-½ tbsp garlic powder

1 tbsp onion powder

1-½ tbsp smoked paprika

1-½ cup non-enriched unbleached all-purpose flour

2 large brown eggs, lightly beaten

2 cups light beer (like Corona Light)

Grapeseed oil

DIRECTIONS

1. Season fish sticks with 1-½ tsp all-natural coarse salt, cracked black pepper, 1 tbsp garlic powder and onion powder. Gently mix well until seasonings evenly coat fish.

2. For the beer batter, in a medium bowl, add flour, 1-½ tbsp garlic powder, smoked paprika and 3 tsp all-natural coarse salt. Mix together until combined. Stir in the lightly beaten egg and whisk in the beer until the batter has no lumps.

3. In a large pot, add about 2 inches of grapeseed oil. Heat oil to about 375 degrees Fahrenheit.

4. Once oil reaches that temperature, dip fish (one piece at a time) into the batter then gently place in the oil. Allow pieces of fish to cook for about 4 minutes or until the fish is golden brown.

5. Place cooked fish on a wire rack to allow excess oil to drain.

6. Immediately serve and savor!

NOTE: Pair with our Family's Secret Tartar Sauce!

Baked Jerk Chicken with Jerk Gravy

BAKED JERK CHICKEN
WITH JERK GRAVY

SERVINGS: 6-8
PREP TIME: 15 MINS
COOK TIME: 1 HR

INGREDIENTS

3 lbs. boneless skinless chicken thighs (remove fat)

2 tsp all-natural coarse salt

½ tbsp + ½ tsp smoked paprika

½ tbsp + ½ tsp French blend herbs

½ tbsp garlic powder

½ tsp cracked black pepper

3 tbsp + ½ tsp mild all-natural jerk paste

3 tbsp extra virgin olive oil

½ medium sweet onion, sliced

½ medium red bell pepper, sliced

½ medium green bell pepper, sliced

1-½ tbsp corn starch

2 cups spring water

½ tbsp gravy master

½ lime, squeezed

DIRECTIONS

1. Preheat oven to 440 degrees Fahrenheit.

2. In a large bowl, add chicken, 1-½ tsp salt, ½ tbsp smoked paprika, ½ tbsp French blend herbs, garlic powder and cracked black pepper. Set aside.

3. In a separate small bowl, add 3 tbsp jerk paste and ½ tbsp olive oil. Mix together and add to bowl with chicken. Mix all together until chicken is evenly coated with paste and seasonings.

4. Add ½ tbsp olive oil to baking dish to coat the bottom before adding chicken. Add seasoned chicken. Bake for 25 minutes.

121

5. While chicken is cooking, in a medium skillet, on medium to high heat, add 2 tbsp olive oil for the jerk gravy. Once the oil is hot, add onions, red bell peppers and green bell peppers. Add ½ tsp all-natural coarse salt, ½ tsp French blend herbs and ½ tsp smoked paprika. Stir well and allow to sauté for about 6 minutes. Stir every 2 minutes.

6. In a large cup, add 1 tbsp corn starch, spring water, ½ tsp jerk paste and ½ tsp gravy master. Whisk together until well combined. Add to the skillet with onions and peppers. Stir and allow for gravy to thicken for about 5 minutes. Turn off heat.

7. Once the chicken is done baking for 25 minutes, add all of the gravy to the baking dish. Bake for remaining 25 minutes.

8. After the chicken is done cooking, squeeze lime over the chicken.

9. **OPTIONAL:** If gravy is too thick, add a little spring water to your liking and stir.

10. Serve and savor!

"The first wealth is health."

—Ralph Waldo Emerson

Classic Family Pepper Steak

CLASSIC FAMILY PEPPER STEAK

SERVINGS: 6-8
PREP TIME: 15 MINS
COOK TIME: 25 MINS

INGREDIENTS

2 lbs. Top Round steak (cut 3 inches long and ½ inch wide)

1-½ tbsp onion powder

2 tbsp garlic powder

¼ tsp cayenne pepper

1 tsp mustard powder

1 tbsp all-natural coarse salt

½ tsp tarragon

1 tbsp, about 2 stems of fresh rosemary, (about 1 tbsp) (destemmed and minced

½ tbsp, about 7-10 stems fresh thyme, destemmed

6 garlic cloves, minced

7 tbsp extra virgin olive oil

1 tsp all-natural red wine vinegar

½ tbsp Worcestershire sauce

½ small, sweet onion, sliced

¾ small red bell pepper, sliced

¾ small green bell pepper, sliced

2 tbsp non-enriched unbleached all-purpose flour

2 cups spring water

1 tbsp distilled white vinegar

1 tbsp all-natural Dijon mustard

½ tbsp Gravy Master

½ lemon (squeezed)

DIRECTIONS

1. In a medium sized bowl, add cut meat, ½ tbsp onion powder, 1 tbsp garlic powder, ¼ tsp cayenne pepper, 1 tsp mustard powder, ½ tbsp salt, ½ tsp tarragon, rosemary, thyme and garlic. Mix together well until seasonings are covered evenly on meat.

2. In a large, non-stick skillet, on medium-high heat, add olive oil. Once oil is hot, add steak mixture. Mix well so that oil covers all of the steak. Stir every couple of minutes.

3. After about 10 minutes of cooking, reduce heat to medium. Add red wine vinegar, Worcestershire sauce, onions and bell peppers. Mix well every few minutes and let it cook for about 10 minutes.

FOR GRAVY

1. In a large cup, add flour and 1 cup spring water. Immediately whisk until flour and water are combined and you see no lumps of flour.

2. Add to cup, vinegar, 1 tbsp garlic powder, 1 tbsp onion powder, Dijon mustard and gravy master. Whisk together well then add to skillet. Stir.

3. Once gravy begins to thicken, add another cup of spring water. Mix well and bring to a simmer.

4. Reduce heat to low. Squeeze ½ lemon and stir.

5. Serve and savor!

"Weight loss doesn't begin in the gym with a dumbbell; it starts in your head with a decision."

—Toni Sorenson

Savory Sunset Curry Chicken

SAVORY SUNSET CURRY CHICKEN

SERVINGS: 8-10
PREP TIME: 15 MINS
COOK TIME: 1 HR

INGREDIENTS

5 lbs. skinless chicken thighs (remove fat)

1-½ tbsp all-natural coarse salt

1 tsp cracked black pepper

1/3 cup extra virgin olive oil

½ large, sweet onion, sliced

1 small red bell pepper, sliced and halved

1 small green bell pepper, sliced and halved

5 garlic cloves, minced

3 medium tomatoes, diced

¼ tbsp fresh ginger, minced

½ tbsp onion powder

½ tbsp garlic powder

½ tbsp smoked paprika

1 tbsp garam masala

2 tbsp curry powder

1 tsp tarragon

½ tsp red pepper flakes

1 cup spring water

1 lemon, squeezed

1 can all-natural coconut milk (13.66 oz)

½ cup of Cilantro, chopped

DIRECTIONS

1. Season chicken with ½ tbsp of salt and 1 tsp cracked black pepper.

2. In large saucepan, on medium-high heat, add the olive oil. Once the oil is hot, add onions, red bell pepper, green bell pepper and garlic. Cook for about 8-10 minutes while stirring every 2 minutes.

3. Add half of the chicken to pot and stir so that most of veggies are on top of chicken. Add remaining half of the chicken on top of veggies. Cover and cook for about 10 minutes.

4. Stir chicken and veggies so the chicken that was on the top, is now on bottom and is able to cook. Cover and cook for another 10 minutes. By now, there should be chicken broth forming in the pot.

5. Add tomatoes and ginger. Stir and cover. Bring to a boil for 5 minutes undisturbed. By now, the broth should pretty much be covering the chicken.

6. Reduce heat to medium. Add 1 tbsp salt, ½ tbsp onion powder, ½ tbsp garlic powder, ½ tbsp smoked paprika, 1 tbsp garam masala, 2 tbsp curry powder, 1 tsp tarragon and ½ tsp red pepper flakes. Stir well.

7. The broth should have thickened. Add one cup spring water and juiced lemon. Stir. Cover and allow to cook for 10 minutes.

8. In a large cup, add coconut milk and whisk until there's no lumps or separation.

9. Add cilantro (to taste) and coconut milk. Adjust salt if needed. Stir well and remove from heat.

10. Serve and savor!

*"Losing weight is a mind game.
Change your mind.
Change your body."*

—Unknown

Family's Favorite Fish Tacos

FAMILY'S FAVORITE FISH TACOS

SERVINGS: 8
PREP TIME: 20 MINS
COOK TIME: 30-40 MINS

INGREDIENTS

5-6 fillets (cut into 2-inch-long sticks)

24 oz. grapeseed oil

all-natural tartar sauce (or our Family's Secret Tartar Sauce recipe)

unbleached, non-enriched tortillas (or our Homemade Flour Tortilla recipe)

all-natural garlic cilantro sauce (or our Garlic Cilantro Sauce)

FOR THE FISH BREADING

1 cup unbleached non-enriched all-purpose flour

¾ cup unbleached non-enriched cornmeal

1-½ tbsp all-natural coarse salt

1 tbsp garlic powder

1 tbsp onion powder

1 tbsp smoked paprika

FOR THE FISH SEASONING

2 tsp garlic powder

2 tsp fresh or ground thyme

1 tsp smoked paprika

½ tbsp all-natural coarse salt

½ tsp cumin

3 tbsp all-natural mustard

3 tbsp all-natural hot sauce

FOR THE PICO DE GALLO

4 medium tomatoes, diced (about 4 cups)

½ medium red onion, diced (about 1 cup)

Handful of cilantro, minced (about 1 cup)

1-2 large limes, squeezed

1 tsp all-natural coarse salt

133

FOR THE SALAD MIX

1-½ cup red cabbage, shredded

1-½ cup romaine lettuce, shredded

¼ cup cilantro (minced)

½ tbsp extra virgin olive oil

½ tbsp white distilled vinegar

All-natural sea salt (to taste)

Cracked black pepper (to taste)

DIRECTIONS

1. Clean fish and cut into fish sticks. Pat dry and set aside.

2. Prepare the pico de gallo. Add tomatoes, red onion, cilantro, lime juice and salt into a medium bowl, mix well and refrigerate.

3. Prepare the salad mixture. Add red cabbage, romaine lettuce, cilantro, olive oil, vinegar, salt and pepper to a medium bowl, mix well and set aside.

4. Prepare the fish breading. Add flour, cornmeal, salt, garlic powder, onion powder, and smoked paprika to a large bowl, mix well and set aside.

5. Season fish with garlic powder, thyme, paprika, salt, cumin, mustard and hot sauce. Mix well to evenly spread over all fish.

6. In a large skillet, on medium-high heat, add grapeseed oil.

7. While oil is getting hot, toss all of the fish in the fish breading, shake off excess flour and place to the side. Do this before you start frying the fish since it only takes a couple of minutes for fish to cook.

8. Once the oil is hot, add fish and cook for about 3-5 minutes on each side. Place on a paper towel to drain excess oil. Continue to do this until all fish is cooked.

9. Spread our homemade tartar sauce on our homemade tortilla. Add a few pieces of fried fish, top with salad mix and pico de gallo. Then squeeze our garlic cilantro sauce on top.

10. Serve and savor!

NOTE: You can use our Homemade Flour Tortilla recipe, our Garlic Cilantro Sauce recipe and our Family's Secret Tartar Sauce recipe.

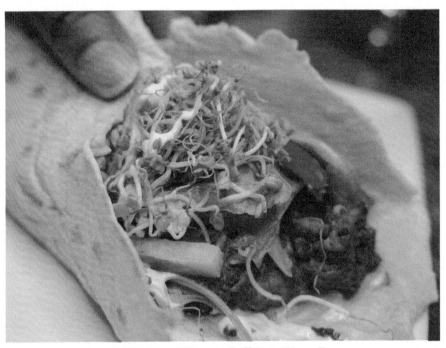

Chicken "Don't Call It a Wrap"

CHICKEN "DON'T CALL IT A WRAP"

SERVINGS: 5-8
PREP TIME: 15 MINS
COOK TIME: 25 MINS

INGREDIENTS

FOR THE CHICKEN

4 chicken breasts, cut into 1-inch squares

8 garlic cloves, minced or mashed in mortar

1/3 red bell pepper, diced

1/3 green bell pepper, diced

½ sweet onion, diced

1 tbsp smoked paprika

1 tsp cracked black pepper

½ tbsp cracked sea salt

½ tbsp Italian seasoning

1 tsp onion powder

4 tbsp extra virgin olive oil or

½ lime, squeezed

FOR THE SALAD MIX

15 grape tomatoes, cut into fourths

¼ bell pepper, sliced (color optional)

handful of Broccoli sprouts

small handful of arugula, chopped

50/50 spring mix and romaine lettuce, rough chopped

all-natural sea salt or coarse salt (to taste)

cracked black pepper (to taste)

FOR THE SAUCE

Natural chimichurri aioli sauce or our The Family's Secret Chimichurri Aioli Sauce

DIRECTIONS

1. Add chicken, garlic, red bell pepper, green bell pepper, onions smoked paprika, cracked black pepper, cracked sea salt, Italian seasoning, onion powder, 3 tbsp olive oil and lime juice to a bag. Mix seasonings well over chicken until evenly coated.

2. In a large non-stick skillet, on medium-high heat, add remaining tbsp of olive oil. Then, add chicken and vegetables from the bag to the skillet. Allow chicken to cook while stirring every 5 minutes.

3. While chicken is cooking, add grape tomatoes, bell pepper, broccoli, arugula, salad mix, salt and black pepper to a mixing bowl. Stir to mix well.

4. To build the wrap, take the tortilla, spread a thin layer of our The Family's Secret Chimichurri Aioli Sauce on tortilla. Top with chicken, then salad mix and broccoli sprouts. Squeeze more chimichurri aioli over the sprouts for even more flavor.

5. Serve and savor!

NOTE: You can use our Homemade Flour Tortilla recipe. Best when using our Family's Secret Chimichurri Aioli Sauce.

BREADS

Cheddar Biscuits

CHEDDAR BISCUITS

YIELDS: 10 BISCUITS
PREP TIME: 15 MINS
COOK TIME: 10-12 MINS

INGREDIENTS

2 cups unbleached non-enriched all-purpose four

1 tbsp raw cane sugar

1 tbsp baking powder

2 tsp garlic powder

1 tsp all-natural cracked sea salt

1 cup all-natural coconut milk

½ cup virgin unrefined coconut oil, melted

1-½ cup shredded sharp cheddar cheese

FOR TOPPING

3 tbsp virgin unrefined coconut oil

½ tbsp fresh parsley, chopped

½ tsp garlic powder

DIRECTIONS

1. Preheat oven to 450 degrees Fahrenheit. Line baking sheet with parchment paper.

2. In a medium bowl, add flour, sugar, baking powder, garlic powder and salt. Mix until well combined.

3. Add melted coconut oil and coconut milk to bowl. Stir well until combined.

4. Add cheese to bowl and gently mix with a rubber spatula until cheese is evenly distributed throughout the dough.

5. Pull apart pieces of dough that are equal to about 1/3 cup and place at least 1 inch apart on baking sheet.

6. Place in oven and bake for 10-12 minutes or until golden brown.

FOR TOPPING

1. In a small bowl, mix together melted coconut oil, parsley and garlic powder.

2. Brush the cooked biscuits with the mixture.

3. Serve and savor!

"Don't dig your grave with your own knife and fork."

—English Proverb

Unleavened Bread

UNLEAVENED BREAD

SERVINGS: 2 LARGE PIECES
PREP TIME: 10 MINS
COOK TIME: 20 -24 MINS (Depending on thickness of dough)

INGREDIENTS

3 cups non-enriched, unbleached, all-purpose flour

2 tsp all-natural cracked sea salt

¼ cup extra virgin olive oil

1 cup spring water

DIRECTIONS

1. Preheat oven to 400 degrees Fahrenheit.

2. In large mixing bowl, add flour and salt. Mix well.

3. Make a hole in the center of the flour, add ¼ cup of olive oil, and one cup spring water. Combine well with a rubber spatula until flour is too thick to continue. Begin to knead with hand until dough is no longer sticky. Put in a sandwich bag and rest at least one hour.

4. Separate dough into your preferred size. Sprinkle a little flour on countertop. Roll out each piece of dough to your desired thickness.

5. Sprinkle a little flour on baking sheet and add rolled dough. Bake for 20-24 minutes. Make sure to not overcook.

6. Remove from oven. Serve and savor!

Homemade Flour Tortillas

HOMEMADE FLOUR TORTILLAS

SERVINGS: 8-12 TORTILLAS (varies based on size of tortillas)
PREP TIME: 1 hr. 5 MINS (or 24 hrs. depending on how long you want dough to rest)
COOK TIME: 2 MINS PER TORTILLA

INGREDIENTS

4 cups unbleached, non-enriched, all-purpose flour

1-½ tsp all-natural coarse salt

1-2/3 cup warm spring water

¼ cup extra virgin olive oil

DIRECTIONS

1. In a medium bowl, combine flour and salt. Mix well.

2. Make a hole in the center of the dry mix. Add the water and olive oil in the hole. Mix together with a spoon or rubber spatula until dough begins to stick together. Then use your hands to knead the dough. You want the dough to stick together but not stick to your hands. If dough is too wet and sticky, add a little bit of flour at a time and knead until dough is no longer sticking to your fingers.

3. Cover bowl with saran wrap and let dough sit on countertop for at least 1 hour. Preferably overnight.

4. Separate dough into your preferred size. Roll into a ball. Sprinkle a little flour on countertop. Roll out each piece of dough to your desired thickness. And sprinkle a little more flour to both sides of the tortilla.

5. Cook on a griddle or large non-stick pan (with no oil) on medium heat. Cook one side of the tortilla for about 1 minute and the other side for about 30 seconds (or until the side is bubbly and has a few brown spots).

6. You can stack cooked tortillas on top of one another. Repeat until all tortillas are cooked.

7. Serve and savor!

Homemade Cornbread

HOMEMADE CORNBREAD

SERVINGS: 18-12
PREP TIME: 5 MINS
COOK TIME: 20-25 MINS

INGREDIENTS

1 cup non-enriched, unbleached all-purpose flour

1 cup yellow cornmeal

2/3 cup raw cane sugar

1 tsp all-natural cracked sea salt

3-½ tsp baking powder

1/3 cup grapeseed oil

1 cup non-flavored, all-natural almond milk or oat milk

1 large brown egg

INSTRUCTIONS

1. Preheat oven to 400 degrees Fahrenheit. Grease your muffin pan or 9-inch round cake pan and set aside.

2. In a medium bowl, add the flour, cornmeal, sugar, salt and baking powder. Whisk to combine well.

3. Make a hole in the center of the dry ingredients and add grapeseed oil, milk and egg. Stir until combined. Do not overmix!

4. Pour the batter into the greased pan and bake for about 20-25 minutes or until the top of the cornbread is golden brown. Poke a toothpick through the center of the cornbread to make sure that the inside is thoroughly cooked. If toothpick comes out clean, the cornbread is done cooking. If the toothpick comes out wet, cook for a few minutes more.

5. Serve and savor!

*"Your body is a temple,
but only if you treat it as one."*

—Astrid Alauda

DRESSINGS, SAUCES & DIPS

Family's Special French Fry Sauce

FAMILY'S SPECIAL FRENCH FRY SAUCE

SERVINGS: 6-8
PREP TIME: 5 MINS
COOK TIME: N/A

INGREDIENTS

1 cup all-natural mayonnaise

1 tbsp all-natural Dijon mustard

¼ cup all-natural ketchup

½ tsp cracked black pepper

¼ cup sweet onion, finely minced

½ tsp all-natural red wine vinegar

DIRECTIONS

1. Mix mayonnaise, Dijon mustard, ketchup, black pepper, onion, and red wine vinegar into a small cup or bowl until they are well combined.

2. Serve and savor!

3. Store in a container of your choice.

Family's Secret Tartar Sauce

FAMILY'S SECRET TARTAR SAUCE

SERVINGS: 6-8
PREP TIME: 10 MINS
COOK TIME: N/A

INGREDIENTS

¾ cup all-natural relish or our Homemade Pickle recipe, minced

¼ cup sweet onion, minced

½ tbsp all-natural mustard

1 cup all-natural mayonnaise

¼ cup fresh dill, minced

½ tsp paprika

¼ tsp cayenne pepper (optional)

½ tsp cracked black pepper

½ fresh lemon, squeezed

DIRECTIONS

1. Add relish, onion, mustard, mayonnaise, dill, paprika, cayenne pepper, black pepper, and lemon in a cup or bowl.

2. Mix all ingredients together until well combined. Serve and savor!

3. Store in a container of your choice.

Garlic Cilantro Sauce (Non-Dairy)

GARLIC CILANTRO SAUCE (NON-DAIRY)

SERVINGS: 1 full squeezable bottle
PREP TIME: 5 MINS
COOK TIME: N/A

INGREDIENTS

1 lemon, squeezed

1 ripe avocado, peeled and pitted

4 large garlic cloves

1 handful cilantro

1 tbsp all-natural siracha, to taste

½ tsp all-natural coarse salt

1 cup spring water

DIRECTIONS

1. Add lemon juice, avocado, garlic, cilantro, siracha, salt and water to blender.

2. Blend for 1-2 minutes or until well combined. Serve and savor!

3. Store in a container of your choice.

Creamy Hot Garlic Vinaigrette Dressing

CREAMY HOT GARLIC VINAIGRETTE DRESSING

SERVINGS: 4-6
PREP TIME: 10 MINS
COOK TIME: N/A

INGREDIENTS

¼ cup extra virgin olive oil

1 tsp all-natural balsamic vinegar

½ tbsp all-natural mayonnaise

1-½ tsp garlic, finely minced

1 tbsp sweet or purple onions, finely minced

1 tbsp red bell pepper, finely minced

¼ tsp red pepper flakes

¼ tsp cracked black pepper

¼ tsp all-natural cracked sea salt

¼ tsp French blend herbs

½ tsp all-natural agave syrup

1 tsp all-natural sriracha

DIRECTIONS

1. In a container of your choice, mix olive oil, balsamic vinegar, mayonnaise, onions, bell pepper, pepper flakes, black pepper, salt, French blend herbs, agave syrup and sriracha together. Make sure to combine well.

2. Serve and savor!

Super Secret Special Sauce

SUPER SECRET SPECIAL SAUCE

SERVINGS: 4
PREP TIME: 5 MINS
COOK TIME: N/A

INGREDIENTS

1-½ tbsp sweet onion, minced

3 tbsp all-natural relish or our homemade pickle recipe, minced

1 garlic clove, minced

½ cup all-natural mayonnaise

½ cup all-natural ketchup

½ tbsp all-natural sriracha

¼ tsp cracked black pepper

DIRECTIONS

1. In a small bowl, add onion, relish, garlic clove, mayonnaise, ketchup, sriracha and black pepper. Stir all ingredients together until well combined. Serve and savor!

2. Store in a container of your choice.

The Family's Secret Chimichurri Aioli Sauce

THE FAMILY'S SECRET CHIMICHURRI AIOLI SAUCE

SERVINGS: 6-10
PREP TIME: 10 MINS
COOK TIME: N/A

INGREDIENTS

1 cup all-natural mayonnaise

1/3 cup fresh parsley, finely chopped

¼ cup cilantro, finely chopped

1 shallot, finely minced

2 garlic cloves, finely minced

2 tbsp all-natural red wine vinegar

2 tbsp extra virgin olive oil

1 tsp red pepper flakes

all-natural sea (to taste)

DIRECTIONS

1. Add mayonnaise, parsley, cilantro, shallot, garlic, red wine vinegar, olive oil, red pepper flakes and salt in a small cup or bowl.

2. Stir all ingredients together until well combined.

3. Serve and savor!

4. Store in a container of your choice.

Homemade Ranch Dressing (Non-Dairy)

HOMEMADE RANCH DRESSING
(NON-DAIRY)

SERVINGS: ¾ CUP
PREP TIME: 1 HR and 10 MINS
COOK TIME: N/A

INGREDIENTS

¼ cup all-natural coconut milk, unsweetened

½ tbsp lemon juice, squeezed

½ cup chilled, all-natural mayonnaise

½ tsp dried chives (rubbed together to make smaller pieces)

¼ tsp dried parsley

¼ tsp dried dill

¼ tsp garlic powder

½ tsp onion powder

¼ tsp all-natural cracked sea salt

DIRECTIONS

1. In a small container or mason jar, add coconut milk and lemon juice. Let sit for about 5 minutes.

2. Add mayonnaise, chives, parsley, dill, garlic powder, onion powder and salt. Whisk to combine well.

3. Close lid tight on mason jar. Chill for at least 1 hour to allow dressing to thicken.

4. Serve and savor!

Israel Family's Herbal Veggie Dip

166

ISRAEL FAMILY'S HERBAL VEGGIE DIP

SERVINGS: 3-5
PREP TIME: 15 MINS
COOK TIME: N/A

INGREDIENTS

2 cups salad mix, minced

¼ cup sweet onion, minced

1 tbsp yellow bell pepper, minced

2 tbsp red bell pepper, minced

1 tsp all-natural sun-dried tomatoes, minced

2 tsp garlic, minced

¼ cup cilantro, minced

1 tbsp all-natural olives, minced

½ tsp red pepper flakes

½ tsp French blend herbs

1 tsp fresh basil, minced

1 cup extra virgin olive oil

½ tsp all-natural balsamic vinegar

1 lime, squeezed

1 tsp all-natural jalapeños or our homemade jalapeños recipe, minced (optional)

½ tsp all-natural coarse salt

½ tsp cracked black pepper

DIRECTIONS

1. Add salad mix, sweet onion, bell peppers, sun dried tomatoes, garlic, cilantro, olives, pepper flakes, French blend herbs, basil, olive oil, balsamic vinaigrette, and lemon to a medium size bowl.

2. Mix well to thoroughly combine.

3. Add salt and pepper to taste.

4. Add jalapenos (optional).

5. Serve and savor!

NOTE: Pair with our Homemade Unleavened Bread. You can also use our Homemade Jalapeño recipe for the jalapeños.

*"It's not a short-term diet.
It's a long-term lifestyle change."*

—Unknown

PICKLING

Family's Secret Homemade Pickles

FAMILY'S SECRET HOMEMADE PICKLES

YIELDS: 6-10 MASON JARS
PREP TIME: 10 MINS
COOK TIME: 5 MINUTES

INGREDIENTS

4 cups spring water

2 cup white distilled vinegar

2 tbsp all-natural cracked sea salt

1 tbsp raw cane sugar

1 sweet onion, sliced

peppercorn (10 per jar)

head of garlic, smashed

bunch of dill

6-10 organic cucumbers (cut off end and cut into spears)

DIRECTIONS

1. In a medium sized saucepan, on high heat, add water, vinegar, salt and sugar. Once the sugar and salt are dissolved, immediately remove from heat. Set aside to allow to cool down to room temperature.

2. Add a few onion slices, about 5 peppercorns, 2-3 garlic cloves and a little dill to each mason jar. Place cucumber spears in the jars. Then, top with more onion slices, peppercorn, garlic cloves and dill. Push the onions, garlic, dill and peppercorns down into the spears/jar if necessary.

3. Once the vinegar water mixture is cooled to room temperature, pour into the mason jars. Fill to the top.

4. Seal jars and refrigerate. They will be ready to eat after 24 hours.

5. Serve and savor!

NOTE: If mason jars are new, make sure to boil jars and lids for a few minutes prior to use.

Homemade Jalapeno Peppers

HOMEMADE JALAPENO PEPPERS

SERVINGS: 2 MASON JARS
PREP TIME: 10 MINS
COOK TIME: 5 MINS

INGREDIENTS

1 cup distilled white vinegar

1 cup spring water

2 tbsp raw cane sugar

1 tbsp all-natural coarse salt

8-10 jalapeños, thinly sliced

4 garlic cloves, smashed

DIRECTIONS

1. On high heat, in a small pot, add vinegar, water, sugar and salt in a small pot.

2. Stir until you see sugar and salt completely dissolve and remove from heat.

3. Fill a jar halfway with jalapeños, add a few pieces of garlic. Fill remaining half of jar with jalapeños and add a little more garlic to top.

4. Slowly pour liquid mixture into each jar until filled to the top. Let jars sit out until it's room temperature.

5. Close lids tightly and refrigerate for 24 hours.

6. Serve and savor!

NOTE: If mason jars are new, make sure to boil jars and lids for a few minutes prior to use.

*"Eliminate the mindset of can't—
because you can do anything."*

—Toni Horton

DESSERTS

Banana Nut Bread

BANANA NUT BREAD

YIELDS: 2 11X6 BREAD PANS
PREP TIME: 10 MINS
COOK TIME: 45-60 MINS

INGREDIENTS

½ cup virgin unrefined coconut oil

1-¼ cup raw cane sugar

1 tsp pure vanilla extract

2 large brown eggs

2 cups all-purpose unbleached non-enriched flour

½ tsp all-natural cracked sea salt

½ tsp baking soda

3 extra ripe bananas, mashed

¼ cup all-natural coconut milk

½ or 1 cup chopped walnuts

DIRECTIONS

1. Preheat oven to 350 degrees Fahrenheit.

2. Add coconut oil and sugar in mixing bowl. Mix on medium speed for about 1 minute or until you see small chunks of sugar.

3. Add the vanilla and eggs. Mix on medium speed for about 1 minute or until well combined.

4. Add flour, salt and baking soda. Mix for another minute or until well combined.

5. In a separate small bowl, mash the bananas. Add mashed bananas, coconut milk and walnuts to mixing bowl. Mix on high for about 2 minutes.

6. Grease two 11x6 bread pans with melted coconut oil with a basting brush. (Be sure to grease all around the inside of the pans to ensure the cake won't stick).

7. Pour half of the batter to one pan and remaining half to the 2nd pan.

8. Place pans in middle rack of oven. Bake for 45-60 minutes. Ensure the cake is cooked all the way through, by poking the middle with a toothpick. If the toothpick is dry, the cake is done. If the toothpick is wet, continue to bake in 5-minute increments until thoroughly cooked.

9. Serve and savor!

*"Eating crappy food isn't a reward—
it's a punishment."*

—Drew Carey

Jacinda's Chocolate Chip & Walnut Cookies

JACINDA'S CHOCOLATE CHIP
& WALNUT COOKIES

YIELDS: 12 COOKIES
PREP TIME: 15 MINS
COOK TIME: 12-14 MINS

INGREDIENTS

½ cup brown sugar

¼ cup raw cane sugar

2-¾ cup unbleached non-enriched all-purpose flour
(for thinner cookies,
use 2-½ cups flour)

1 tsp baking soda

¼ tsp all-natural cracked sea salt

1 large brown egg

2 tsp pure vanilla extract

1 cup virgin unrefined coconut oil, softened but not melted (for thinner cookies, use 1-1/3 cup oil)

1 cup semisweet chocolate chip morsels

½ cup chopped walnuts

DIRECTIONS

1. Preheat oven to 350 degrees Fahrenheit.

2. Mix brown sugar, raw cane sugar, flour, baking soda and salt in a medium bowl.

3. In the same bowl, add egg, vanilla extract, coconut oil. Mix well.

4. Fold in chocolate chips and walnuts.

5. Portion out 12 cookies and roll them into a ball shape. Place them on a cookie sheet, lined with parchment paper, and bake. (Give each cookie a little space to spread when baking).

6. Bake for 12-14 minutes.

7. Remove from oven and allow to cool. Serve and savor!

Non-Dairy Donuts

NON-DAIRY DONUTS

SERVINGS: 12 DONUTS
PREP TIME: 1 HRS and 45 MINS
COOK TIME: 20 MINS

INGREDIENTS

1 cup warm spring water

½ cup raw cane sugar

2-½ tsp all-natural instant yeast

¼ cup grapeseed oil

2-¾ cup non-enriched, unbleached all-purpose flour

½ tsp all-natural cracked sea salt

DIRECTIONS

1. In a medium bowl, add warm water, sugar and yeast. Mix until sugar is dissolved.

2. Add grapeseed oil, flour and salt. Mix with a rubber spatula until the dough begins to form. If the dough mixture is too wet, add a little more flour at a time until the dough is not sticky.

3. Knead the dough on a lightly floured surface for about 5 minutes or until the dough is smooth. Shape the dough into a ball.

4. Grease a large bowl. Add dough to greased bowl and move the ball of dough around to grease the dough all over.

5. Cover the bowl with a towel for 1 hour to allow dough to expand.

6. Push the dough down with your fist to let out the extra air.

7. Place the dough on a lightly floured surface and mash it in a round, almost flat shape with your hands. Create a log shape by stretching out a large hole in the center of the dough. Cut the log of dough into small pieces. Size will vary based on how big or small you want your donuts. (Normally yields 12 pieces)

8. Shape each piece into a ball, then flatten each piece with anything hard and flat that you have (ex. bottom of a plate, donut cutter, etc.)

9. Poke a hole in the middle of each flattened piece of dough using a bottle cap or a piping bag nozzle. Set the dough from the bottle cap to the side.

10. Make all of the dough that was set aside from the bottle caps into one ball. Flatten, and poke hole in that one for one more donut.

11. Cover the donut pieces with a towel and let it rest for 20 minutes. After the 20 minutes, the donut pieces should have risen a little.

12. In a large skillet, on medium to low heat, deep fry the donut pieces until the bottom side is golden brown. Flip to the other side and fry until golden brown.

13. Remove from oil and set fried donuts on a cooling rack.

14. Dip the donuts in whatever topping you'd like. (Ex. powdered sugar, cinnamon sugar, fudge, etc.)

15. Serve and savor!

"Success is the sum of small efforts, repeated day-in and day-out."

—Robert Collier

Homemade Fudgy Pecan Brownies (Non-Dairy)

HOMEMADE FUDGY PECAN BROWNIES (NON-DAIRY)

SERVINGS: 16 BROWNIES (IN A SQUARE BAKING DISH)
PREP TIME: 15 MINS
COOK TIME: 25-30 MINS

INGREDIENTS

6 tbsp virgin unrefined coconut oil

4 ounces bittersweet chocolate morsels

1/3 cup all-natural plant-based milk (ex. almond, oat, walnut)

1 tsp pure vanilla extract

¾ cup unbleached, non-enriched, all-purpose flour

1 cup raw cane sugar

¾ cup unsweetened cocoa powder

¼ cup brown sugar

½ tsp baking powder

¼ tsp all-natural cracked sea salt

2 large brown eggs, beaten

½ cup chopped pecans or walnuts

DIRECTIONS

1. Preheat oven to 350 degrees Fahrenheit. Coat an 8 or 9-inch baking dish (preferably square) with a little melted coconut oil to prevent sticking.

2. In a small saucepan, add half of the chocolate morsels and milk and place on low heat. Cook and stir for about 2 minutes, then add the coconut oil. Continue to cook and stir until oil and chocolate have melted. Remove from heat and stir in vanilla.

3. In a large mixing bowl, combine the flour, sugar, cocoa powder, brown sugar, baking powder and salt. Mix well.

4. Pour the chocolate mixture into the flour mixture and stir until combined.

5. Add the beaten eggs, remaining chocolate morsels and ¼ cup of the pecans or walnuts. Stir to combine.

6. Pour the batter into the greased baking dish and sprinkle top with remaining pecans or walnuts.

7. Bake for approximately 25-30 minutes. At 25 minutes, poke the center of the brownie with a toothpick to see if the center is cooked all the way. If the toothpick has a small amount of fudgy crumbs on it, then the brownie is done. If the toothpick comes out completely wet with batter, bake for additional time.

8. Remove from oven and allow to cool for about 10 minutes before cutting.

9. Serve and savor!

"Please test your servants for ten days:
Give us nothing but vegetables to eat and water
to drink. Then compare our appearance with that of the
young men who eat the royal food, and treat your
servants in accordance with what you see.' So, he agreed
to this and tested them for ten days. At the end of the
ten days, they looked healthier and better nourished
than any of the young
men who ate the royal food."

Daniel 1:12-15 (NIV)

German Chocolate Cake

GERMAN CHOCOLATE CAKE

SERVINGS: 15
PREP TIME: 30 MINS
COOK TIME: 45 MINS

INGREDIENTS

FOR THE CAKE

2 cups raw cane sugar

1-¾ cups unbleached, non-enriched all-purpose flour

¾ cup unsweetened cocoa powder

1-½ tsp baking powder

1-½ tsp baking soda

1 tsp all-natural cracked sea salt

2 large brown eggs

1 cup all-natural coconut milk

½ cup grapeseed oil

1 cup boiling spring water

2 tsp pure vanilla extract

FOR THE COCONUT FROSTING

½ cup light brown sugar

½ cup raw cane sugar

½ cup virgin unrefined coconut oil

3 large brown egg yolks

¾ cup all-natural almond milk

1 tbsp pure vanilla extract

1-½ cup chopped pecans

1-½ cup all-natural shredded coconut

FOR THE CHOCOLATE FROSTING

½ cup virgin unrefined coconut oil

2/3 cup unsweetened cocoa powder

3 cups all-natural powdered sugar (use coffee grinder and

grind raw cane sugar to make powdered sugar)

1/3 cup all-natural almond milk

1 tsp pure vanilla extract

DIRECTIONS

1. Heat oven to 375 degrees Fahrenheit. Grease two 8 or 9-inch round baking pans with a little melted coconut oil. Cut a round piece of parchment paper for the bottom of the pan to assure the baked cakes will not stick.

FOR THE CAKE

1. In a large mixing bowl, add sugar, flour, cocoa powder, baking powder, baking soda and salt. Stir well.

2. In a separate medium bowl, combine the eggs, coconut milk, oil and vanilla and mix well.

3. Add the wet ingredients to the dry ingredients and mix to combine.

4. Add the boiling water and stir. The batter will be very thin.

5. Pour batter into greased baking pans.

6. Bake for 25-35 minutes or until a toothpick inserted in the center comes out clean.

7. Allow cake to cook for about 15 minutes before placing them on cooling racks.

FOR THE COCONUT FROSTING

1. In a medium saucepan, on medium heat, add brown sugar, cane sugar, coconut oil. In a small bowl, whisk egg yolks and almond milk. Add egg mixture to the pot. Stir well and bring to a low boil. Stir continuously until the mixture begins to thicken.

2. Remove from heat and stir in vanilla, pecans and coconut. Allow to cool completely before adding frosting to cake.

FOR THE CHOCOLATE FROSTING

1. Melt coconut oil and add to a medium mixing bowl. Stir in cocoa powder. Add powdered sugar and almond milk. Beat on high speed until the frosting can be spread around cake easily. Add more milk to thin the frosting or more powdered sugar to thicken it.

2. Stir in the vanilla extract.

FOR ASSEMBLING THE CAKE

1. Place one of the cake rounds on a plate or turntable.

2. Spread a thin layer of chocolate frosting over top of one layer of cake. Then spread a thin layer of half of the coconut frosting over the top of the cake.

3. Stack the second cake on top of the bottom cake. Spread chocolate frosting over the entire cake.

4. Spread the remaining coconut frosting on top of the cake.

5. If you have any chocolate frosting left, you can use a piping tool/bag to decorate the edges of the cake.

6. Serve and savor!

Chocolate Brainiac Snack

CHOCOLATE BRAINIAC SNACK

SERVINGS: 9x13 baking pan
PREP TIME: 10-15 MINS
COOK TIME: 5-10 MINS
CHILL TIME: 4 HRS MINIMUM (Preferably overnight)

INGREDIENTS

9 oz. all-natural dark chocolate morsels (the higher percentage, the better for your brain)

1 tsp virgin unrefined coconut oil

12 oz dates

1 cup all-natural almond butter

½-1 cup chopped walnuts

3-½ tbsp all-natural light agave

¼ tsp all-natural coarse salt

DIRECTIONS

1. In a small saucepan, on medium-low, add chocolate morsels and coconut oil. Allow to melt down slowly while occasionally stirring.

2. While the chocolate is melting, remove the seeds out of the dates. Make sure dates are fresh and there are no signs of mold in the center.

3. Lay dates down flat (skin-side down) on a piece of parchment paper placed inside of a 13x9 inch glass baking pan.

4. Place another piece of parchment paper on top of the dates and use something hard (ex. rolling pin, back of plate, bottom of cup) to flatten dates.

5. Remove top layer of parchment paper and pour spreadable almond butter across top of the dates. (If almond butter is thick, melt until it's a spreadable consistency).

6. Sprinkle chopped walnuts evenly across almond butter.

7. Once chocolate is melted, add 2-½ tbsp of agave and stir. Then, pour evenly across the walnuts until there's a thin layer covering the entire surface.

8. Sprinkle sea salt across the chocolate.

9. Place in the fridge for at least 4 hours (preferably overnight) before serving.

10. Cut into squares, serve and savor!

NOTE: Dark chocolate and walnuts stimulate neurological growth in our brain, so this is a healthy snack that could also make you smarter.

FINAL WORDS FROM JABEZ

I'd like to take this opportunity to recognize my father, Toney Singletary. He is hands-down the biggest influence and inspiration behind my cooking abilities. If it weren't for his guidance in the kitchen, I would not be the chef I am today. I love you Dad!

In closing, I feel it's important to note again, that this cookbook was designed to reflect the principles that I explain in "Life Matters So Let's Eat Like It!" If you have a goal to lose weight, and you have not read the book, I suggest grabbing a copy. When you understand the information in the book and you apply it while cooking the meals in this cookbook, you will be equipped with an awareness of how to choose the right versions of the food you like to eat, while shedding your unwanted weight at the same time. The truth is, once you understand these principles, you can apply them to literally any recipe that you find online or in any other cookbook for that matter. It's unfortunate that we have to be so intentional about the foods we choose here in the states, but this is our reality.

It is my goal to inspire as many people as possible to practice the principles of eating natural ingredients, but more importantly to choose to make this a lifestyle. In other words, make a decision to only eat amazing natural foods that our bodies are compatible with… FOR LIFE! Consistency is key! For those of you that do take on this permanent mindset shift and make these choices consistently, the only thing that I ask is once you get the results and these recipes are ingrained in your mind, that you would pass these books along to someone else you know who has a goal to lose weight.

My brothers and sisters, I love y'all!

Prayers Up Blessings Up!

"Then God said, 'I give you every seed-bearing plant on the face of the whole earth and every tree that has fruit with seed in it. They will be yours for food.'"

Genesis 1:29 (NIV)

IN MEMORY OF

This cookbook is dedicated to our grandparents that have passed on. My grandma Delois actually passed away a few days before writing these very words.

The love and the flavor that we put into every meal that we prepare for our family is a reflection of all of you as well as all of our ancestors, going all the way back to the beginning of time. There are no words that can explain the level of love, respect and appreciation that we have for all of you!

We know that you're watching over us in spirit. Please continue to guide us. We pray you know it is our intention to make all of you proud.

Prayers Up Blessings Up!